The Frugal Millionaire Mindset
written by Christine Szakonyi

Copyright 2021 by Krisztina Anna Szakonyi, Christine Szakonyi

Cover Photo Credit: Krisztina Anna Szakonyi

Cover Design: Krisztina Anna Szakonyi and Emese Simon

Edited by Emese Simon, www.emesesimon.com

First published: 2021

ALL RIGHTS RESERVED NO PART OF THIS BOOK MAY BE REPRODUCED IN ANY FORM WITHOUT THE WRITTEN PERMISSION.

Contact: thefrugalmillionairemindset@gmail.com

YouTube: Puzzle Gain

YouTube Link:

https://www.youtube.com/channel/UC-xO3nMmj9ovzGAl2BXn6SA

Instagram: Frugal Millionaire Mindset

Instagram Link: https://www.instagram.com/frugalmillionairemindset/

Facebook: The Frugal Millionaire Mindset (Page)

Facebook Link:

https://www.facebook.com/The-Frugal-Millionaire-Mindset-104513261731865

Dedication

For my parents and my lovely grandmas.
Hálás köszönet szüleimnek és nagymamáimnak.

I want to thank Gavrilo with all my heart for teaching me the mindset of a frugal millionaire.
Nek padaju ljetne kiše po nama.- Lexington, Ljetne kiše

Table of Contents

CHAPTER ONE 1

THE TRUE STORY BEHIND THE BOOK 1

CHAPTER TWO 16

THE HARD WAY OF LEARNING FINANCE 16

    Repeating bad patterns 17
    Not making the effort 18
    Toxic feelings 19
    Focusing solely on money and burning out....................20
    Time killers, Social media & Co. 22
    How I made the change...24

CHAPTER THREE..27

THE EASY WAY OF LEARNING FINANCE..........27

    Have the right attitude 28
    Stay calm and learn from the mistakes of others 29
    Decision making techniques..30
    Be reliable! 31

CHAPTER FOUR...33

TAKE CONTROL OF YOUR SPENDING...............33

    Frugal is not a four-letter word...34
    Frugal Millionaires don't always start at home 34
    Implement your own ideas...35

Watch every penny! 36
Live below your means 38
Don't try to live up to the expectations of your family and friends 39
Track your expenses 39
Homework 40

CHAPTER FIVE 42

THE ZERO WASTE 6 R SUSTAINABILITY PYRAMID 42

1. Rethink / Respect everything around you 44
2. Refuse to spend on all that is unnecessary 44
3. Reduce your shopping for daily items and think in bulk 46
4. Rehome your items 47
5. Reuse what you can 49
6. Repairing and Repurposing your stuff is cool 50
Consider Minimalism 51
Homework 51

CHAPTER SIX 52

HOW TO TURN YOUR PENNIES INTO MILLIONS 52

The magic of Compounding Interest 53
What is compounding interest, and why is it going to blow your mind? 54
How long do you have to keep investing? 55
Mastering the right moment 56

CHAPTER SEVEN 58

SOUL BEFORE MONEY 58

Make your health a priority 58
Avoid burnout 59
Choose wisely 60
Staying calm 61
Work when others relax, enjoy your time when they panic 62
Life is beautiful 63

CHAPTER EIGHT 64

LIFE PARTNER AND PERSONAL RELATIONSHIPS 64

Self-development comes before relationships 64
Life Partner 65
Grow up to greater tasks 66
Learn who you can trust 68
Friends 69
Your Environment 69
Homework 71

CHAPTER NINE 72

MISTAKES TO AVOID 72

Learn how to say NO 72
Don't put all your eggs in one basket 74
Getting through hard times 75
Homework 76
Know your boundaries 76
Envy and Long-term habits 77
Trying to impress others might kill your plans 78

CHAPTER TEN 80

SZAKONYI'S FRUGAL MILLIONAIRE CAKE 80

What does a portfolio mean from the frugal millionaire mindset perspective? 80
- 1. Emergencies: 6 Month Reserve 81
- 2. Knowledge..81
- 3. Courage..82
- 4. Surviving Crises.....................................82
- 5. Care and development 83

CHAPTER ELEVEN 84

PRIORITIZE AND FOCUS 84

Write down your ideas 84
How to prioritize...85
What can be done?..85
Eisenhower Matrix 85
Homework..86
1. Section number one is the Urgent-Important box. 87
2. Section number two is the not urgent, but important box. 88
3. Section number three is the urgent, not important box. 89
4. Section four is the neither urgent-nor important box. .90

CHAPTER TWELVE 91

YOU HAVE EARNED YOUR MONEY, WHAT'S NEXT? 91

So how can you eliminate these bad patterns and become a happy millionaire?..92
Non-material elements...................................93

CHAPTER THIRTEEN 94

LESSONS SUMMARY 94

- The Hard Way of Learning Finance 95
- Easy way of Learning Finance 95
- Take control of your spending 95
- 6Rs 96
- How to turn your pennies into millions 96
- Soul before money 96
- Life partner and personal relationships 97
- Mistakes to avoid 97
- Szakonyi's Frugal Millionaire Cake 97
- Prioritize and focus 97
- You have earned your money, now what? 98
- Closing thoughts 98

Preface

Being yourself and remaining true to yourself is a real challenge these days, especially when you work hard to achieve financial freedom as a young adult. Is there a magical spirit that surrounds the self-employed mindset, or is there something more to discover? What are you looking for at all? Could you describe it?

Tons of books offer you the ultimate recipe on becoming financially independent and successful, but nobody can guarantee when or that you'll ever even get there. And the reason for that is that most of the books offered by the finance-advisory market concentrate mainly on how to turn yourself into a millionaire instantly. They don't focus on many of the essential lifestyle choices we should make in order to become financially independent. It's not easy to figure out how to achieve financial success -as being successful means entirely different things, even to two best friends. However, having a positive mindset is fundamental in reaching your goals and creating your destiny. But there are several other vital parts and factors of your life which have to be managed, focused on, and continuously improved.

I highly recommend this book to all young ambitious people who want to take control of their financial destiny early on in life, avoid making crucial mistakes, and to build wealth regardless of their earning potential at their jobs.

I also recommend it to more experienced individuals who are not afraid to listen to the real-life experiences of a young frugal woman. I only ask you to be open-minded and enjoy my honest way of writing. Furthermore, I genuinely hope you will find this book useful and mind-blowing, and this journey of development will motivate you to step into the world of finance or help you move further on your life-path whenever you feel you are deeply stuck. Never forget, you only have one chance to live an extraordinary life. Let me help you get there.

The Frugal Millionaire Mindset
written by Christine Szakonyi

A first-hand account of a young village girl on her journey to becoming a frugal master in finance.

Chapter One

The true story behind the book

My story began just like a Hollywood fairy tale where the poor young girl meets a wealthy man, and they live happily ever after. My happily ever after remains to be seen, so far so good, I will keep you updated! :)

I grew up in a lovely little village in Hungary, where time has stood still since the 1990s. It's a place where the old-fashioned way of life still exists and everyone has something negative to say about other people's goals and ideas, and everyone seeks everyone else's approval of their personal lives. But instead of paying any attention to my surroundings, I minded my own business and I stayed off the beaten path.

I grew up fearing money, and as a teenager it was challenging to understand the world of finance. I saw two completely different approaches to money. My dad was a frugal and extremely hard-working bricklayer, while my mom was a nurse who, at that time, spent most of the money on me and private classes. My mom cherished me because my older sister had passed away when she was 13 months old, and this had made my relationship with my mom quite unique. My parents and grandparents were overly lenient with me growing up, and my mother's helicopter parenting style turned me into an uncaring teenager.

Breaking out of this box and achieving my goals was not an easy task, and it took a long time to discover my real passion. In the past I had always hovered near poverty and what changed me was falling in love with the most principled man I have ever met, who transformed my way of thinking about what success, wealth, and value really meant.

With his mentorship I blossomed from a country bumpkin to a financially responsible adult within few years. Since then, that poor girl from the beginning of the story had become the practitioner of the frugal millionaire mindset.

It is rewarding to be able to teach people about wealth, principles, and becoming financially independent. It gives me such joy to be helping not only young people, but the older generation as well, who should listen to me carefully with open ears, because my results are extraordinary, despite my young age. Why do people believe that what I say is real and possible to achieve?

I spent 19 years in the educational system that was supposed to prepare me for life, however, I was already an entrepreneur at the age of 18. That's how I started to humbly push myself and study harder. I am an economist with a Master's degree in Finance, but I have several other professions too (I stopped counting somewhere around ten) and I define myself as a kind of renaissance woman. I courageously moved abroad alone at the age of 22 and experienced life challenges such as work and finances first hand. After moving to Vienna, I learned an entirely new language (German) within three years while writing my master's thesis about cryptocurrencies in English. Just a few days after my arrival in Austria, I started working as a waitress and quickly adapted to the new lifestyle. By now I can speak three languages fluently, and I believe that everybody can change, rethink, or improve their lives just as I did. I spread positive energy and take advantage of all new opportunities to make peoples' financial lives better. My YouTube channel is called Puzzle Gain where I have easy and clearly formed lessons about the concept of the frugal millionaire mindset and cryptocurrencies. I am so passionate about these topics that I spread the knowledge both in English and Hungarian for my natives to overcome the language barrier. I go the extra mile to create videos in two different languages, but that's what being driven means. But my mindset had not always been like this. I failed English after my first semester in high school, and I was one of the worst performing students during the first three years. I was only interested in parties and didn't care about the future. However, at the age of 16 I experienced a life-changing event. An ice skating accident turned my life upside down, and the concussion I suffered changed my priorities, my behavior, and my entire attitude towards life.

My mother was dumbfounded when she saw me studying for my history exam for eight hours straight. She could hardly recognize her daughter. I know only a handful of people who worked and studied as much as I did in my final year of high school. This change in my attitude and the work ethic I adopted led me to this point, where now I help everyday people every day to get a handle on their money, pass down my knowledge of finance and cryptocurrencies, and I am on my way to become an international author.

By the time I moved to Austria I had realized that hard work paid off in other places on the planet too, not just in Hungary. Within three years, I got my Master's degree in Finance. But fate had other surprises in store for me, and I ended up meeting an amazing man and eventually ended up living in his villa in Vienna. But it was not at all what you might think…

This relationship started as many romantic relationships begin nowadays, on Tinder. I had just downloaded the app and we matched. To be honest, I swiped his profile right, only because he had a single photo of him on a motorbike in front of a stunning landscape which appealed to me. At the time my German wasn't that good yet, so we chatted in *"Germish"*, our special mixture of English and German. After a while, I gave him my phone number and he called right away, insisting on seeing me the very same day. I told him as I had already had plans, but he turned up outside my workplace anyway, and the next thing I knew it was one o'clock in the morning, and he was taking me home to my flat, after having talked through the night. Then he kissed me and told me he was falling for me, and I must admit, I had butterflies in my stomach. His name was Gavrilo.

Soon I would find out where he lived. The first time I visited his house, a big villa in an illustrious neighborhood of Vienna, I was a bit intimidated as I had never seen anything like that before. As I entered, my first question was, who cleaned this colossal house? I was so naive, so inexperienced, and still just a little village girl back then. He just laughed, and still often recalls this moment.

He inherited the giant villa from an elderly millionaire who was like a mother to him. Ms. Annie had a miserable childhood and six siblings, but ended up marring a wealthy man whose family owned property investments in Vienna. She met her future husband on a cold, rainy night, after finding out that her boyfriend had been cheating on her. She was sitting on a bench at the railway station, waiting for the first train back to Vienna, when a handsome tall man in a nice suit offered her his jacket. They talked all night and got married within a short time. He was the one who introduced her to the frugal millionaire mindset.

Ms. Annie never wanted to have children, because she thought that having children cost too much money. Which sounds funny coming from a millionaire, but that was her opinion. Even though she never became a mother, later on in her life when she met Gavrilo, she looked at him as her own grandson and took him under her wings. It all began when Ms. Annie hired Gavrilo at the age of 19 to do chores around the mansion during the summer break of 2001 while he was visiting his relatives in Austria. Then, in 2006 she hired him for a permanent full-time position as her personal assistant and chauffeur. Over the years they grew to be close companions, and after she had taught him to speak perfect German, she began to mentor him about finances, investments, and most importantly, taught him the frugal millionaire mindset. Gavrilo spent long faithful years in her service until the end of her life, and she left him the villa with all its contents in her will.

Ms. Annie's estate included several millions of Euros, and a lot of other assets and properties. So believe me, I had the opportunity to learn indirectly from a real millionaire. My love story with Gavrilo, a man who had such a large and valuable inheritance, with whom I had much in common with, enabled me to gain knowledge in the world of finance that I never would have been able to otherwise, which I hope to pass down to you in this book.

I do not know exactly why fate has put me on this path, but in retrospect I can say that it was the perfect way for me to understand what a real millionaire mindset meant. With Gavrilo's help, I was able to transform my old mindset into a new way of thinking at a young age. Nowadays, I often hear from people in their 40's and 50's that they wish they had my mentality, back when they were young, because if they did back then what I am doing now, they would be happily retired millionaires by now.

I experienced real wealth first hand, living in an illustrious part of Vienna, and as a village girl I realized what the upper-class lifestyle truly meant, and how the 1% managed their lives. This experience and financial knowledge opened my eyes to an entirely new perspective that I never would have been able to understand without these factors being part of my life for several years.

Of course, I realize that my story is unique, and this factor will be absent from the lives of most people. But that is exactly why I am writing this book, to share with you all the methods you too can use in your life in order to be on your way towards financial independence.

I've learned more about money from Gavrilo than from any book, and I used this knowledge in my own life to get successful and reach my burning desires. When a person comes from poverty, they deal with things in a completely different way than people who come from more privileged backgrounds. Gavrilo, who had experienced both wealth and, destitution and war, often told me, that he had no money for two pairs of cheap shoes, and he was right. Now, neither do I, just for one good pair.

Now you might say that you won't take advice on frugality from a woman who has been living with a millionaire in his villa for years, who has no everyday problems, doesn't have to pay rent, has no expenses, and you think it is easy for her to talk. You probably assume that I am a sugar baby and receive thousands of Euros in allowance. But you couldn't be more wrong. You see, things weren't really what they seemed at first, and even though he did own a villa, he was not doing well financially at all. But I stayed with him anyway because I fell in love with him and felt that he was right for me, regardless of his income at the time.

I want to share some stories with you so you can understand what we actually went through with Gavrilo and how we took control over our financial lives both as a couple and individually. When I met Gavrilo, I was already living on my own and worked hard for my money as a waitress, and I also cleaned properties as a side hustle. My record was 26 days of work without a break at three different places, and I cried myself to sleep every night because I was so homesick. I earned my money the same way you do, with sweat and tears, the hard way.

When I met Gavrilo he was in a much worse financial situation than he is now, and we've developed our finances together over the course of our relationship.

So now you are wondering, how come he was not doing well when I met him? Well, because inheriting a huge house doesn't come with a pocket full of money. What it does come with are extraordinary expenses.

Gavrilo would have had the opportunity to inherit millions from Ms. Annie. Her family had been neglecting her for years, only Gavrilo had been there for her. For a long time, she hesitated between leaving her entire estate to Gavrilo over her nephew. A few days before her death, she had her banker give her nephew some of her funds. Fearing that it would be all he'd get, and she'd change her will, he had her declared incompetent. When she realized what he had done, she refused to eat anymore and left this world sadly. Although she was no longer entitled to make changes in her will, Gavrilo stayed by her side until her last moment. The dying woman's family showed little regard for her and only turned up at the very last minute. In the last few days of her life, she expressed her regret to Gavrilo several times for not having left him her entire fortune. Ms. Annie realized she had made a huge mistake by hesitating. Her fortune ended up going to her nephew who had just used her. But the wonderful life she had lived gave her peace at the end.

At the time Ms. Annie died, Gavrilo not only worked for her, but also had a business that went bankrupt within a few months. So he had not only lost tons of money, but also the income he had been receiving from her. He did have money saved, after all, he was in possession of the frugal millionaire mindset already. But the sudden loss of income and the expense of the house spiraled him into a negative state of mind. He was mourning the loss of his dear old friend, and on top of that, people close to him envied his inheritance and turned against him. What followed were several years of hardship. Because he had been in a domestic personal service for several years, it would have been difficult to return to a conventional job without further education. So he went back to school, all the while paying for the expenses of living in Vienna out of his savings.

Gavrilo had been living with his girlfriend for sixteen years, and they broke up six months before I came into his life. He was going through a challenging period when I met him. He got a part-time job, and in the first few months I actually made more money than he did.

It never occurred to him to sell the villa or any of its furnishings to make his life easier, even though I often encouraged him to do so. But he had different ideas and I had to accept them, even though it upset me because I didn't understand his way of thinking. He had stable principles, and the house meant too much to him and he was never going to sell it.

By the time Gavrilo met me, he was already desperate, not just because of his finances, but because a part of his life was missing. This piece of the puzzle was true love and partnership, which turned out to be me. Together, we rebuilt everything technically from zero, using the frugal millionaire mindset.

We both developed ourselves very quickly, and we supported each other through this journey, which sometimes included painful and difficult times.

Since we both have strong personalities with entirely different cultural backgrounds, we often had passionate arguments. Still, at the end of the day, we always found the way back to each other. We are not only a couple in love, but best friends too. The principles he had taught me made me a better person, and I was able to subdue the untamable lion.

His goal was to get me out of the waitress job and have me find a job that was better suited for me since I already had a degree in economics. I completely agreed, because I was unhappy being a waitress, even though I earned quite well with tips. I felt like I wasn't living up to my potential, and watching the patrons coming into the pub in their nice suits day after day, filled me with envy.

Three months into our relationship, we went on a budget holiday to Greece, and that trip was a turning point for me. I left as a waitress, and came back as a person with renewed goals. I went on temporary unemployment and got €400 a month, and I decided that the first step was going to be perfecting my German, so I enrolled in a course and Gavrilo, who by now spoke perfectly practiced with me patiently every day. I literally spent every single minute of my life learning German, and I was improving rapidly. In the meantime, I applied for several office jobs, but they wouldn't hire me because speaking German well wasn't enough, I had to have an official certificate. In Austria, they are very uptight about having the right certificates and titles for job positions.

Losing my waitressing income made me very depressed, and I often wanted to just go back, but Gavrilo wouldn't let me. Even though I cried my eyes out, he stuck to his guns that I should persevere, he kept telling me that giving up was not part of our dictionary and that I needed to keep applying for office jobs and push myself even harder and time would solve everything.

He supported me lovingly while at the same time, having been in the service, trained me with his military style. This was strange to me because my parents had raised me completely differently. I was an only child for a long time (after my sister had died at the age of one), so my parents let me do anything and everything, and I became a spoiled brat who hung out with the wrong crowd. I had an absentee father who worked abroad, so my family model didn't include a dad who sat at the dinner table every night.

Gavrilo's background is completely different, he comes from a close-knit family. This kind of closeness was almost foreign to me, as if I had a hard time accepting that there were actually well-functioning families out there. So we had many differences, like two poles of a magnet who were attracted to each other.

During our first year together, one bad thing happened after another. He also became unemployed, so including my unemployment check we only had €1400 a month. His mom was being treated for cancer at that time, so there was a lot of turmoil, plus additional expenses. We were so broke, by September we were freaking out about how we were going to pay for the heating in the villa the coming winter. Living in a freezing mansion turned out to be just as unpleasant as it sounds. There is nothing like going to the toilet in 13 degrees Celsius in the middle of the night.

I felt so unsuccessful and felt so sorry for myself that all I could do was lie in bed and cry. I was depressed, negative and volatile. At some point we even had to borrow money, which took over a year to pay back. I felt ashamed to heat the house on borrowed money, but feeling warm again was lovely.

During this time I came to realize that I wasn't the only one lost in the dark. Gavrilo hadn't found his path yet, either. He was getting more dissatisfied as the days passed, started gaining a lot of weight, and he was always tired.

By the time I finally got my German language certificate it was already spring. I sat on the marble steps of the house for a long time, crying tears of joy. Soon after that I found a well-paying job after a year of struggling.

Within a few months I already knew that I wouldn't keep that job forever, like the people who had been working there for

20 years, and doing the same thing day to day would not fulfill me in the long run. The idea of having job security was nice, but I was too ambitious, and wouldn't settle for a fixed but limited salary. So I decided that no matter how much time it took, I would do whatever I had to in order to reach my goal, which was to work in finance. So, with a stable but limited German knowledge I applied to a 2-year master's program in 2018, while still working full time.

When the lovely professor asked me during the interview why I believed that I could finish the program, I enthusiastically replied with tearful eyes, *"Because it is my responsibility to finish everything I start. I will continue to improve my German every single day. And even though I have a full-time job, I will get my degree within the time frame of the program, because I have done this before. I had worked and studied at the same time before back in Hungary, and if I could manage that, I can manage this school as well, if you just give me a chance."*

And what do you know, within a few days I got accepted to the program. The first semester was quite difficult, because university level German and English finance jargon were new to me. On top of that, I was working as a multi-lingual sales assistant at the time, plus learning Serbian from Gavrilo. So for six months I was pretty dizzy from all the languages, and by the end of the day I didn't even know what I was actually speaking. I had to work twice as hard as the other students to eliminate the German and English language barrier, while my classmates only had to deal with English. But it seemed the pressure was too much, because many of them left the program after a few months.

For a long time I was embarrassed to present and speak in front of natives and especially professors due to my insufficient German knowledge. I don't know if there is anyone out there who could be real confident being in the spotlight in front of dozens of people, after having learned German for less than a year, not even knowing all the basic words, let alone presenting at university level. Austrians spoke way fast too for me with their heavy Viennese accent. I would concentrate on my mistakes and felt that people didn't understand me. During this hard time, I found a new friend in a lovely girl who attended the same program. She had Hungarian roots, but grew up in Austria. We decided to do a language exchange. I taught her Hungarian, and she helped me to speak and think in German.

When our financial situation started improving with Gavrilo, we decided not to upgrade our lifestyle. This was key to our future success. So we pretended that we only had the 1,400 Euros a month like we had over the past year. We began to invest the rest of our earnings little by little. Gavrilo told me incredible stories about the time he spent 6,000 Euros a single night when he was younger. To think that we were not earning that much together in a month bothered me a lot. It often upset me that he refused to sell this property because it was worth so much, we could have lived happily ever after for the rest of our lives, without ever having to work again. Everyone has dreams. Mine was a quaint country home and a nice sports car, and Gavrilo's dream was to travel the world in a catamaran. We could have fulfilled both of our dreams instantly, but instead we continued to work, searched for opportunities, and we found a way out.

Gavrilo decided to get into cryptocurrencies in 2017 when the big explosion took place, and many people invested in it. We didn't actually buy any cryptocurrency at that time directly, but Gavrilo is good at I.T. and he built a mining rig. We invested our excess income into paying the electricity to sustain the mining system. (If you don't understand what a mining rig is, you can find out in my second book.) I was sometimes confused whenever he would come home with 60 gaming cards, but he always managed to make new rigs. I didn't mind because the cards give out a lot of heat, and heat was something we definitely needed in the house.

I supported his dreams, I didn't overspend, and eventually started to invest with him together.

I became an enthusiast in 2018 even though I still had no idea how cryptocurrencies worked. I just sent him money through my bank account with the comment *"I love you"*, and he bought Bitcoin. He realized the big potential in the technology, and he became my bull, whom I supported. He made me so curious that I opened my own cryptocurrency wallet, and I ended up writing a master thesis about Cryptocurrencies.

From 2018 on when I started my part-time master's studies in finance, I intensively developed my financial skills as well, and I ended up being a diamond hand at investing. At the beginning we were only interested in cryptocurrencies but later also invested in vintage watches, antique objects, and many more to create a more secure portfolio.

So, this is the story of how we rebuilt our life together from zero to a 6-digit amount within three and half years. It was Gavrilo's principals and my compliance to learning and putting the effort into bettering myself that made it happen.

When someone is born into a well off family, it is much harder to learn the value of things, and rich kids often forget about or underestimate real values.

Appreciating things comes naturally when we have experienced going without. Unfortunately, the school curriculum doesn't include helping us recognize the importance of financial independence. Life has other ways to teach us, harden us, and make us determined and strong.

Before writing this book my personal goal was to have a finance-related profession, and now, with a Master's degree in Finance and Economics, I have the confidence to guide you through my own life experiences. Though I am not a financial advisor, I offer you this book as a guideline in finance. However, you must take responsibility for your own financial decisions, as all the money you invest is your own risk or gain. This book is based on my path and personal experiences and I can promise you that it is not one of those written about 'How to set up your first drop shipping website or YouTube channel'.

The frugal millionaire mindset is based on self-development and financial improvement. It is about a way of thinking, giving you long-lasting and lifestyle changing advice on how you can learn from the prosperity and difficulties of others, how to handle them with a kind of positive financial mindset and how to prepare yourself and get through the hard days. With all this knowledge, you can reach your set goals much easier.

My aim is to help people become more future-oriented and financially independent. These two key points can lead you to happiness and help you reach your life goals faster than you'd expect. Through necessary financial stability, you can become more relaxed and less stressful. You might not consider yourself to be a materialistic person, but still you need money for your daily groceries. Let's face it, you can't be happy if you are hungry. With the help of more money and stabilized finances you can buy better quality food, so technically you could buy yourself longer life-expectancy.

Moving in the right direction, reaching financial freedom, and creating your own success story day by day is not always easy, I know. The beginning is very tough for most of us. My path had also been filled with countless obstacles, and I'm sure that I am not the only one. These experiences and the knowledge I have gained, enabled me to believe that I can support you on your journey if you are willing to come along with me. I am here to show you that you have to be your own priority, you are your own best friend, and that you can reach your financial goals if you are willing to work for them. You won't get there without making a serious effort, but I can show you the way. I hope you will heed my advice, and become a frugal millionaire.

Chapter Two

The hard way of learning finance

Before you build a new house, you must demolish the old one, and clear the way. In this chapter, we'll go over some attitudes and habits that must be eliminated from your life, so you can forge ahead with a clean slate.

Repeating bad patterns

I think we all have a family member or a friend who has an enormous debt or an extremely badly organized financial life. Yes, that one! Week after week they go on borrowing money from friends or the bank, or if they do have money, they spend it on frivolous purchases. Why don't they ever learn? Well, that is what I call the *"Hard way of learning finance."*

These individuals cannot learn from their own mistakes. You think you can change and motivate them, because they appear very positive at first, and you can see a momentary passion in their eyes, a sign of some sort of change. But a day later they forget all the lessons, they change their minds very quickly, and go back to their comfortable overspending ways. Instead of setting a long-term financial goal, they want to have that brand-new TV for 5,000 Euros to take home in their leased cars while smoking cigarettes on the way. They will act the same way tomorrow and every single day after that until it is too late.

It's a pattern similar to dieting. *"I will start tomorrow."* **But they never actually do.**

They want instant gratification from the *"small box"*. Becoming financially independent is the most challenging box to break—the box of self-control. It's a kind of human weakness. You can't start a *"financial diet"* with the help of the frugal millionaire mindset and then expect results if you eat chocolate all day. You must make the effort.

Not making the effort

If you have recognized yourself in the never starting diet example above, if you are motivated for a minute, but never actually start the diet, please don't worry, it's absolutely normal. Please do not close this book so quickly, because if you feel that you want to change, you can. But not without making an effort!!!

By nature, we are designed for survival and most of our behavior is instinctual. It is extremely difficult to do things that you are neither in the mood for, nor do you see immediate gratification. We handle short term stress much better, and that's why long-term achievements are challenging tasks for the human brain. It is coded in our evolution. This is the reason why you procrastinate doing things that you find exhausting, tedious, and obsessive, and you promise yourself to do it later. **Everybody has bad days, it's natural, but if you feel down from Monday to Friday then you are technically under the weather more than 70% of your life.**

There are low moments in our lives, and going through these experiences is a part of life. Having some bad days or even a longer period of time is totally acceptable, but it can't go on forever, and you can't use them as an excuse to postpone taking serious steps to change your life. At some point you have to face your challenges head on, make the effort, and stick to your decision.

Toxic feelings

I deeply respect all the religions, but they rarely focus on having an instantly good life. I highly appreciate your beliefs, whatever they may be, and I hope you are on your way to spiritual happiness, but I want you to cherish the belief of the possibility of an instant good life. In this case, we are talking about your finances and mental well-being.

There are some people who always talk about their sad childhood experiences, and whenever you see them you only hear their negative thoughts related to money, their fears, jealousy, or pettiness. Even the weather seems to be against them along with everything else. After meeting them, you feel like you need to take deep breaths to get rid of all their negative energy, but even hours later you feel dizzy and innervated. Sounds familiar?

You simply cannot imagine changing your life for theirs, not even for a day. Some individuals are simply unable to manage their financial lives, and they transmit negative energy even if you show them a way out. But there are some people who laugh all the time and always show their best face, which sometimes is just a mask, and they hide their real feelings, which is just as harmful as if they were depressed.

Every single day, you have 24 hours, and how you spend them is in your hands. You can sleep 13 of these hours or just 8 or even 6. Regardless, I am here to give you warnings to WAKE UP. Not only in finance, but also in your general mentality, because these two things go side by side. Mental health is indispensable for making serious effort, and it translates to a healthy financial life as well.

Having toxic feelings about yourself or the world around you is a kind of mental self-destruction. This is something I also went through when I felt hopeless in my teenage years. When you feel that your burdens are too heavy to carry, you use any excuse not to change your life.

I'm sure you have often told yourself that it's impossible to achieve your goals for one reason or another. Maybe you simply hate Mondays and feel happy only on Fridays and at the weekends. What's even worse is that you haven't set a life goal and a bucket list, so technically you have no idea what you want to achieve in the upcoming five years.

What would you tell yourself if you knew that you would die within 365 days? How would you spend the last year of your life? If your answer is *"Hell… well… not like I do today!"* then this is the right time for change!

Focusing solely on money and burning out

Positive thinking and mindset in the western culture is a new science which we have just started getting a taste of but haven't been able to adapt to well, so as soon as a single cloud covers the sun we are already heartbroken.

Technically, focusing only on money in a book and getting an instant millionaire mindset is not enough to become financially independent. It's way more complicated, so that's why I give you simple examples. The solution is tricky because if you only run after money you might burn out, or you already have, and you can easily lose your mind.

Burning out means not enjoying your hard-earned money as you should be. Working and pushing yourself hard become meaningless, even if you get to check your fat bank account day after day. Yes, you heard me well, if you are burnt out you are afraid to spend your money at your own pleasure. The hard way of learning finances means that you can ONLY learn from your own mistakes. It is based on your general understanding. We often fail to learn the lesson the first time and keep driving along the wrong but well known road again and again. But in business, you have to stand up and learn from your mistakes. Try not to take the negative energies from your last projects and financially unlucky incidents with you. Can you imagine a CEO or CFO crying over a bad financial decision and staying at home for weeks without going for the next business opportunity? This kind of behavior would cause enormous damage to a company.

So why don't they follow this pattern that ordinary people do? Because nowadays, the world is changing fast and there is no time to cry over spilled milk. Those who are bold enough to push the gas pedal in the fast lane are watched by jealous eyes of those who don't dare to drive faster than 60 km per hour. These brave ones are able to react quickly and figure out the best strategies and scenarios in order to influence their future. They are not perfect, and they also make mistakes, but with the ability to learn from their mistakes, they can drive further on their own journey. Learning from the most solution oriented people and making an effort to find the best scenarios is always the right decision.

Time killers, Social media & Co.

It's a cliché, but very important to remember. Nowadays, we are literally attached to our mobile phones. Phones are handy tools. We store our entire lives on our phones; bank accounts, bookings, orders and shipping info, messages, Christmas photos, videos from our kids, personal calendars, e-mails. Have you ever thought what would happen if you lost your phone? It would feel like you have lost a piece of you, and you'd insanely search your home to find it. If you are a social media type, you might sometimes feel that you have wasted a whole hour/afternoon/day/weekend scrolling the news on your Facebook wall or checking Instagram, maybe TikTok. But even if you are not a social media user, you watch YouTube, play games, read some forums or watch movies all night. Or you have a TV which is on loud when you are at home, and you watch your favorite series all the time. These are real time wasters. If you want to be successful, you need to prioritize. If you have a mission, you can't fulfill it by being lazy. Having a millionaire mindset, you need to be frugal with your free time. Our social lives have changed a lot, but it's better to concentrate on having quality times with your real friends. Focusing on three hundred Facebook friends is not possible, and at the end of the day, it doesn't matter who had more likes on their profiles. Society now measures success with likes, but you need to remember that this is only an illusion. You can do it, but only for fun, but you can't measure your personal value through likes. You can check on your phone how much time you spend on social media. If it is high, like 5 hours daily, you need to rethink whether this adds real value to your life or is it just a waste of your time, and you'll end up complaining to your acquaintances that you have no time.

Sometimes we are jealous of people who have enough time to do things we don't, but we don't realize that the times which we spend with lazy activities, they use for their own success.

Be honest with yourself. Are you on social media too much? How could you make your time more productive on Facebook? You might get some fresh ideas to join in groups that help your financial development. Social media is the gem of community building. You can connect with people of similar interests in a matter of seconds, and you don't have to wait for a face-to-face meeting. You can get information and knowledge you never would have thought of in seconds. Instead of browsing the timeline or pictures on your phone before going to bed at night, think about what useful hobby you could start that would take your financial development forward. The platform is not the real problem, it's about learning to use it correctly. Social media platforms are beneficial things. You can see your friends' and family's profile and check to make sure that everything is fine, and share your important moments. But do you use social media only for fun and watching cat videos? How do you select the content that you consume?

If you fill yourself with negative news and spend your time listening to conspiracy theories, it will consume a lot of your energy, which has a diminishing effect on your financial success because you put yourself in a negative mindset. If you are on social media, you need to take the time to unfollow all opposing feeds, that rob you of your time and make you feel confused, envious, or unhappy. Find yourself new positive groups and people to connect with. These are the steps to take, to reform your bad habits. But you have to start with yourself first in your development.

This is not just about social media but also other bad habits that take a lot of time away from us. You need to understand that you need to use your free time in a way that makes sense, and that opens the possibility of ideas to flow into your life.

Development often takes a lot of energy. I know that there may be moments when you feel like you are unsuccessful and that you can't move anymore. But this is the moment when you have to go and find yourself, despite the fact that weakness and exhaustion are parts of your self-development. Remember that financially successful people are not happier than you, but more principled, and they have learned to fight harder. Feel rich and relaxed for ONE DAY, but remember the NEXT day you need to speed up!

How I made the change

As a young child, I was a terrible student, and I often cheated on school tests because I had no motivation to learn. In hindsight, I see that the problem was that I didn't know how to learn back then. I was young and only wanted to play like every other child. There was nobody around to teach me that learning could be playful. I can remember one summer when I was 10 we had to read a 700-page book. I only read every tenth page because I despised reading books. My parents hired tutors for me, so I wouldn't fail my exams. My mom was disappointed in me because my grades were so poor, and I felt ashamed. But at the same, time I tried all kinds of extracurricular activities. I was on all the sports teams, did some excellent school projects, but nothing caught my interest for more than a few weeks.

When I was 16, I was so lost that I planned to skip high school altogether and move abroad to earn some money as a maid or waitress in hotels. I was going to move to Austria's ski resorts in Tirol to make enough money, so later I could move back and buy myself a house in Hungary. This was the only idea I could come up with at the time, but I had no real goals or passions. When I explained my plans to my parents, they wouldn't hear of it. Clearly, they didn't allow me to skip school and my dad was adamant that I should finish high school. This made me very upset, and I kept resenting going to school until my ice skating accident happened. I had a head injury and was hospitalized for two weeks. The accident made me realize that if I kept cheating on school tests I wouldn't learn anything, so in essence I'd be wasting all of my time. I started to study and worked hard to prepare for my next history test. I remember how my school performance improved as my self-motivation and life goals changed. I began to study hard, but I had no passion for anything, and even after that life changing accident these aimless feelings often reoccurred until I turned 22. But still, I pushed myself harder and harder. I became a perfectionist, yet working and studying didn't help me find my path. Until university, I did everything the way I was supposed to, without cheating on my exams.

But I learned my life lessons the hard way at university. Once I had a lousy study group to work with, and we cheated. I wasn't going to take part in it, but the others made me, and I didn't have the willpower to say no. I also wanted to help them and be a team player. The professor realized what we had done. The others tried to cover their tracks, but I was honest and took all the blame. I apologized which the professor accepted, because he appreciated my ethical behavior, and we all ended up passing at the end of the semester. We all make bad decisions in life, but it comes down to how often we repeat them and how we eliminate them in the long term.

Nowadays, as a young adult, I realize that back in those days it was me who created the boundaries of what I could or couldn't achieve, and I only behaved as a mirror of the world I had experienced. I was profoundly influenced by my hostile environment. With time, we all become wiser, and the sooner we realize that we must destroy our boundaries and reshape ourselves, the sooner we can obtain a better life. The earlier we wake up the faster we can change the course of our financial direction.

You have no idea how many people I've met in their forties and fifties who have expressed regret about having lived a hedonistic lifestyle without thinking about the future. Please remember something important, if you are older. It is never too late to change. So free yourself from your mental boundaries. Ninety is the new sixty. You are still young.

Chapter Three

The easy way of learning finance

Whatever your purpose is in life, you have to be crystal clear about it and put it down on paper, otherwise you can easily get sidetracked.

Finding something you can feel passionate about makes achieving it way easier. For a very long time I was also living my life without any goals and visions until I realized what I was passionate about. Success is much easier when passion is involved. If you are able to put together a vision of who you want to become, don't hesitate to go for it, but remember it is hard work. First, you should figure out how you can you accomplish it. Nobody can make this plan, but you. When you are able to come up with a plan, you have already created a visible way to move forward and achieve it. But remember what my wise grandma once said, *"You can only save money when you have it, and the most difficult thing is to keep it. Spending it takes a blink of an eye, but then you'll have no resources to achieve your next, bigger goal."*

Have the right attitude

Which one of your imaginary glasses did you put on this morning? The dark ones that make everything seem negative, that show the world as a horrible place, and your life as awful? Or the bright ones, which show you that your life is beautiful and full of possibilities, solutions, and inspire you to keep moving further on your path?

Treat yourself with positive thoughts because, if you surround yourself with negativity, then you will have no spiritual strength to move forward and achieving your goals will seem impossible. The first step is having the willpower to change. On one hand, you can't expect other people to change your life and help you through difficulties. On the other hand, it is challenging to have a positive outcome from negative thoughts. When it comes to financial improvement, open-minded thinking is critical, because otherwise you will block your own ideas. It is human nature to blame other people when we fail, when we are not willing to take responsibility for our mistakes, or when we are unable to leave certain life circumstances without getting hurt. Learn from your past mistakes and believe in your future luck. There is nothing else you have to do right now, besides focusing on the positive side of life and working hard for your goals. Forget the word *"problem,"* never even start a sentence with 'the problem is' and instead concentrate on the solutions.

Negative attitudes are widespread nowadays, and I've met many wealthy people with a negative mindset. You can be rich and full of negativity, but I assume that these people in general didn't become rich by working joyfully or by expanding their opportunities. They gained wealth in a brutal way, with sweat and tears, and they have issues, like living in constant fear of losing their money. They are not frugal millionaires, but the thorny millionaires.

Stay calm and learn from the mistakes of others

If there is a hard way of learning, then there should be an easy way of learning as well. As my wise grandma always used to say, "The stupid learn from their own experience, and the wise ones just watch the stupid, and learn from their mistakes." How genius was my dear grandma's simple explanation on learning the hard way about life and finances.

In other words, don't keep repeating the same mistakes all the time and try to learn from the experiences of others. Of course, it's easier said, than done. Giving advice to others is always easier because you see their situation from an objective point of view. But if you are at the center of the problem, you might not realize it, let alone find the best solution. Solving your own issues always seems more difficult and sometimes even impossible.

There are certain professions like being a surgeon, a judge, a politician, a pilot or an investor, in which you are forced to make fast decisions, and you are not allowed to make any mistakes, otherwise you will have to pay the consequences. These mistakes could change your financial stability by losing your license or reputation. I want to remind you that patience is an excellent tool in eliminating mistakes in life, financial mistakes included. So, if you have a short amount of time to make a decision, I recommend that you take a deep breath and count to ten. If you are already trained to make decisions within seconds, then it might be harder for you to remind yourself of the ten-second rule.

Decision making techniques

1. If you are in a stressful situation, you must count to ten and take some deep breaths. Only give answers and make decisions afterwards.

2. It is always best to sleep on a big decision, whenever you have the chance. Sudden decisions can lead to mistakes. You will see things from a different perspective with a fresh mind, or else, and you might regret your hasty choice.

3. Another simple way that will help you with your financial decisions is to actually gain a deep, clear, and broad understanding of finance. Use your free time to learn about finance, read books just like this one or watch YouTube videos on this topic.

4. The field of investments is a vast topic, and you need to understand the basics, such as how to create a portfolio and the psychology of investments. You can try anything that you find inspiring or financially promising, but before you act, you need to invest enough time to understand exactly what to do.

5. The Don't Panic Method simply means that you don't sell out of panic- AND DO NOT LISTEN TO YOUR FEARS. If it seems that you are losing money one day, don't panic, you might triple it the next day. Patience and being educated in the topic is essential, and nobody will learn it for you.

Be reliable!

If you want to be financially successful you have to become the person you yourself would love to do business with. Keep in mind that no matter what your business is, bad news about you and your business always spreads quicker than good news. If you don't behave correctly in business, your business partners will inevitably disappear.

Let's take an example. You have a meeting with a partner or partners. Don't get frustrated if you're late for an appointment, but make sure to call and notify them, because wasting their time not only looks bad on you, but it makes them impatient and judgmental. This small gesture reinforces your credibility. Of course, there are instances in life which we can't avoid that make it impossible to inform the members of the meeting in a timely manner. In this case ,never forget to apologize and always give the reasons for being late. Learn to BEHAVE AS A RESPONSIBLE ADULT.

Investors and customers look for companies, and people whom they can confidently place their money with. Business is not only about finances, but also about trust.

So stay reliable all the time, arrive on time, finish projects on time, and communicate any changes in the project that might cause delay or any other alterations. You need to learn to communicate as a reliable and trustworthy person in order to gain more business opportunities in the long run. Always remember, the greater the trust, the more deals you will secure. Your word is your bond.

Chapter Four

Take control of your spending

Your goal is to build wealth, even though you don't make extraordinary amounts of money at your job. You simply cannot imagine how someone like you will ever have hundreds of thousands or even millions in your bank account. You know that it takes money to make money, but you have none of it. So obviously, the first step is to save up some capital. In this chapter, I will show you what you can do to establish your capital, by adopting the frugal millionaire lifestyle and attitude.

Frugal is not a four-letter word

The word *"frugal"* has a negative connotation. Let's face this demon, this word that you don't want to become, because you think if you commit to this path, from this day forward you will have to give up everything that you love, and you will be miserable for 30 years. Let me guess... the words you associate with frugal are: cheap, raggedy, low quality, old, worn, giving up on any sort of fun, no holidays, no goodies... hmm, am I close?

Being a frugal millionaire doesn't mean that you have to go without having nice things. Let's stick with the coffee example. Let's say you are a big coffee drinker, and you spend too much money on this habit. Invest into a beautiful thermos that you will love to drink your coffee out of every day, and from that point on, make your own coffee. Your image doesn't have to suffer. You can be stylish, environmentally friendly, and save money and resources simultaneously.

Adopt this mindset into all areas of your life, and you will create the foundation of a more secure life. All it takes is a goal, and the willpower to see it through.

Frugal Millionaires don't always start at home

Home. Your lovely, sweet and cozy place. No matter where or who you live with in this world, whether you live alone or in a big family, this is your base. There are certain things you bring from home, things you've experienced, the way your parents lived. It may be that your parents had bad financial habits and that is all you are familiar with.

I have good news for the young readers who still live at home. When you leave the nest, you can choose what to do with your own life, and do not necessarily have to follow in your parents' footsteps. You can simply change the pattern because it is not the only way to live.

Implement your own ideas

I personally hate watching television. Ever since I was young, I remember having to watch my favorite series, and having to endure 10 minutes of brainwashing advertisements. I recognized early on that I didn't want anyone to tell me which shampoo or toothpaste to use. I didn't want to be influenced, and I didn't want to spend twice as long watching a movie. After I moved out I left watching television behind and switched to YouTube instead, which is a modern miracle. You can find all kinds of information there, but you need to take your time to discover some excellent role models. Also, learn to control yourself and watch only meaningful content. I won't recommend any channels because if I got started on that, this book would never end. We all have our own tastes, and we enjoy watching different topics and content creators. Choose someone who helps you and motivates you in your finances, and you will learn a lot from them. Moreover, you don't have to accept your parents' other habits either.

Let's start with everyday routines. Don't go to the shops every day as your mom did. Do your shopping weekly, because it's cheaper than going daily because you won't get lured into spending your money on all the special offers, and you will get more free time too. I never understood why my parents used to buy only one package of coffee and cause themselves weekly stress over the next life-saving portion. If it is something that you need regularly, then start purchasing in bulk. Watch the special offers, think of winter clothes at summer and vice versa.

Watch every penny!

Why don't you buy second-hand clothes, since they are much cheaper and better for the environment, and most of them are still practically new? The money you save this way can go towards your investments. Has your dad ever changed light bulbs for environment-friendly and long-lasting energy-saving ones? Do it in your own home. Or perhaps your parents bought a refrigerator on credit? Then, definitely do the opposite. Buying a used one is more budget-friendly. Don't mind what others say, clean it properly, and it will serve its purpose. There is a lot of stuff for free or for very little money that you can find in Facebook groups, at garage sales, on specialized web-pages or simply on the street nicely packed up. Whenever I find something useful, I pick it up without feeling any shame. I never thought I was too good to use my hands to clean it, even living in a villa, if it meant saving money. I got my vacuum cleaner free, second hand and it works just as well as a brand new one. Create yourself surplus money for your investments over and over again.

Big dreams that have come true had all started with small steps like closing a dripping water tap. Dare to take small steps. You have to locate the areas where cash flows out of your pocket. Before making a purchase, check if there is a possibility to get the item second hand, or just be patient and wait for a good deal. It never ceases to shock me when people tell me about the credit card debts they have accumulated due to their spending habits. Please heed my word and don't allow yourself to become a purchase junkie. In this chapter, I must mention subscriptions too.

They are wallet killers, so subscribe only if it's something that you use on a regular basis and cancel them once you stop using them.

For example, if you often order from Amazon, then having a prime membership is a good investment, so you can save on shipping costs. But if there is a page that you haven't even logged into for two years and your membership fee is taken automatically from your account, then it's time to cancel that subscription.

Wake up, the time to become a frugal millionaire is NOW. Take your time to pick up these second hand goods for free or almost free. You need to think of it as a sustainable way of life that will help you achieve your financial goals. You will keep a much more significant part of your earned income and create some capital, and that will make you proud of yourself. If you live in an environment where using used items is unacceptable, you need to check if you are at the right place. Buying yourself new things might make you feel good right now, but saving some extra capital will provide you with more freedom in the long run.

Unplug everything that you don't use. It can save you up to 30% on electricity. On one hand you save energy, on the other hand you can invest this extra money in your future. Invest in an energy-saving light-bulb and enjoy the long-term benefits. Don't let the water run too long, keep your showers short, you won't be any cleaner, however you waste valuable water. Keep water-usage low in the kitchen as well. There is no place for wasting resources and money. If you do a little calculation, you will realize that letting the water run every single time for 20 seconds adds up to a lot. You waste hundreds of liters of clean water every month which you never actually use but nevertheless you must pay for it.

Don't buy new and expensive designer items. A lot of young people like to be fashionable and show off their newest brand name outfits. You would be shocked if you added up the value of all wasteful purchases that only end up collecting dust on a shelf once they go out of style. Don't do that. Avoid all the temptations of all unnecessary shopping. Other bad habits that cost a lot of money are smoking, drinking in bars, and collecting things that have no potential to turn into an investment.

Live below your means

How much you earn is not the only factor that determines how much you'll save. It is your lifestyle choices that will make the ultimate difference.

To become a frugal millionaire you need to strive to keep your expenses low even if you could afford a higher living standard. As human beings we believe that when we earn more we deserve more, and we want to quench our thirst with a bigger car or a bigger house. But we often forget that these purchases are long term decisions. Upgrading your lifestyle means that you will never have enough cash reserve, in case of inflow cut. Remember, people with increased income often fall into the debt spiral.

Let's take an example of two people who earn different amounts. X earns 2,000 a month, Y earns 4,000 a month. X has a roommate, drives a used car, cooks at home, so on, and saves 300 per month. Y lives in a larger apartment, leases a car, has high insurance, goes out dining regularly, buys designer clothes and not only does he not save, but accumulates credit card debt. Meanwhile, X saved 3,600 a year while Y paid for his lifestyle choices. If X loses his job he will have the safety net of approximately 2 months of paychecks. But, when Y loses his job, it will be a very painful situation, because there will be no emergency package to live the same lifestyle.

Do you live beyond your means? How much money could you save if you moved to a different neighborhood or apartment? Do you drive a car that you can't afford to impress others or make yourself feel better about your life? Be honest with yourself when you answer these questions.

Don't try to live up to the expectations of your family and friends

Your family and friends might suggest that you take on a loan or credit after college even though you haven't even started paying back your student loan. They may believe that you should buy a big house, a nice car, as part of your social status. Before making this decision consider whether you really want to run into the mousetrap like 90% of people do.

Let's take the example of cars. If you buy a low-budget car which you can afford without a credit, then it will give you an advantage in the long run. Take into consideration factors like the cost of insurance, the size of the gas tank and the cost of yearly service. So you should reduce the number of your insurances to the minimum, keep only the most essential insurances and basic driver's coverage. This also means you have to drive more carefully, and avoid getting tickets of all kinds. You can convert the money you saved this way into your dreams, financial education, business, stock or other long term investments.

Track your expenses

When I was 18 years old I didn't have as much money as I wished I had, and I overspent on unnecessary items to make myself feel better, and I often felt guilty for not saving enough money. When I started tracking my expenses in the first year, I couldn't believe my eyes.

I spent 4,000 Euros on nothing of remarkable value within that year. Many people struggle with emotional spending. Having a lack of self-control and stopping the habit of overspending is quite challenging. Over the years I have become better and better at tracking my daily incoming and outgoing expenses, and after three years I no longer had to keep doing it. Don't worry, you don't have to do it for the rest of your life, either. After a while, you will learn from your mistakes and start making better decisions in your everyday spending. Take some time at the end of the month to do a success list.

How much money will you end up saving by not buying unnecessary things? If you are not determined enough, you won't be able to build any capital. Sometimes you need to feel the pressure of your financial plans on your shoulders, or you will never be able to move forward. Home is the first place where you have to be strict with yourself, and you have to set common goals with your partner or your family. I will talk about relationship goals in a further chapter.

Homework

Your task now is to start tracking your expenses including all your fixed costs and variable costs. Be honest with yourself. Get a blank piece of paper or start an Excel file. If you have a family account with your partner, then use it as a family expense tracker. In the first column enter your monthly income and in the other column enter your fixed monthly expenses such as rent, phone bill, insurance, fuel, food and everything that is necessary for living. Subtract your fixed costs from your earnings. Whatever remains could either be saved or spent, which makes it variable.

Is your wallet always empty at the end of the month? What mistakes do you keep repeating? What are you doing wrong? What are your variable expenses? In other words, beyond your bills, what do you spend your money on?

In economics a company has fixed and variable costs. Your personal budget works just like that. You cannot change your fixed costs in a short term, but it's manageable if you do some research and make some effort. It's more important to check your variable costs. Let me explain in simple terms what variable costs could mean. Feeling like you can't live without buying the fifth pair of shoes within the season? This is emotional spending for things you don't really need. You need to make sure that your variable expenses are really worth it or are unavoidable. Once you significantly lower your variable expenses, you can start your savings with little resistance.

Chapter Five

The zero waste 6 R Sustainability Pyramid

Zero wasters have become my role models through their philosophy. I have been a vegetarian all of my life, and I feel that we need to be more responsible. We should care about our environment, save resources, but since it's a book about finance, let's not forget how expensive meat is. I hope to not only turn you into a frugal millionaire but also a person who cares about their environment, and through being mindful about the implications of what you spend your money on, protect the Earth for our great-grandchildren.

Zero wasters are incredibly talented at spending minimal amounts of money. The book Zero Waste Home by Bea Johnson has helped me to understand what to do differently at home, so I implemented some of her suggestions into my finances and I have been enjoying the benefits ever since.

Now I will explain the zero waste 6 R Sustainability Pyramid. I will not talk about the additional 3 Rs the Restore, Recycle and Rot, but I think these are very important too and if you are motivated enough feel free to do your own research and read about them.

Here are the 6Rs:

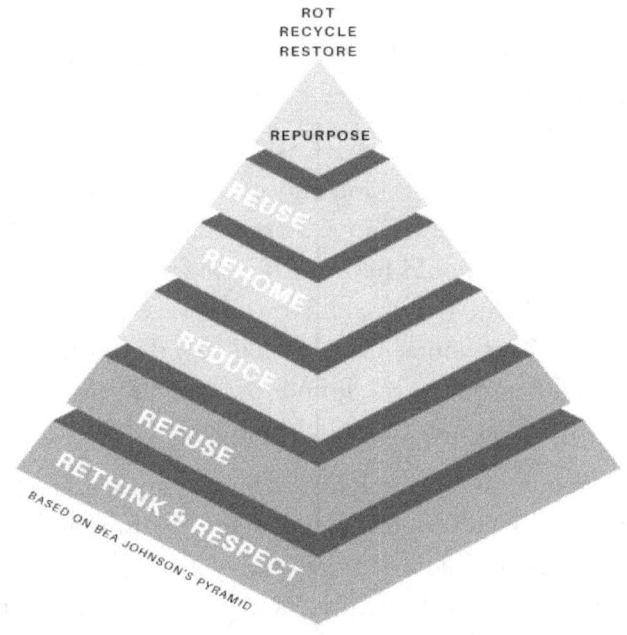

1. Rethink / Respect everything around you

The first and foremost thing to realize is that we have only one planet. Most resources are non-renewable, and we have to handle them carefully because if we damage our world irreversibly there will be no reason to save money. There will be no place to spend it. Frugality is not only about saving money, but also about creating a sustainable way of living in order to save our planet. Our home, Earth, should always be our first priority.

2. Refuse to spend on all that is unnecessary

The *"Refuse to spend"* principle is what you have to keep in mind in order to become a frugal master.

Before making a purchase ask yourself, *"Do I really need this item?"* Give yourself some time and wait at least one day, even if this item costs only a few Euros. Start making a list of all the random purchases you would have made, and add it up at the end of the month. With this new habit, you will save massive capital in the long term. Test yourself, and you'll see, if you take a look at your list in a few months, you'll find that you have forgotten about most of those items, and you didn't really need them after all.

Buying new things might make you happy temporarily, but if you check your household you can see the mountain of items just collecting dust. Like a little squirrel, you keep collecting things that are simply not worth the price and your home is becoming an unorganized nest. The reasons for ninety per cent of your shopping are your impulsive emotions and the lack of willpower, and the remaining ten per cent is what you need to have for a fulfilled life. Sticking to your principles and refusing to spend on unnecessary items is a challenging, but necessary habit to become a Frugal

Millionaire. This way you become not only a frugal person, but a friend of zero wasters and our planet too. Zero Wasters care about plastic waste, and you care about financial waste using their methods.

These are such simple habits to adopt into your lifestyle that you won't even realize what a good a person you have become while saving money. I try not to go anywhere without my water bottle, so I don't have to spend money on plastic bottles, which cost a fortune. My coffee cup is almost always with me with coffee or tea in it and if I need a second one, I will get it cheaper in my own mug instead in a plastic or paper mug. I will present you the figures below. Let's go over your weaknesses and let the math persuade you.

Let's take one very simple example. A beer or coffee in a pub costs around 4 Euros. (When doing your math, use figures that apply to you.) If you go out five times a week, then your coffee or beer costs you 20 Euros a week.

Multiply this by 52 weeks in a year, and the sum is 1,040 Euros. In a single year you spend 1,040 Euros only on a cup of coffee or a beer which in ten years' time is 10,400 Euros. It is an incredible amount of money, don't you think? If you prepared your coffee at home you would save about 60 to 80 % of that amount.

What about ordering takeout for 20 Euros three times a week too? It's 60 Euros a week which comes to 3,120 Euros a year and 31,200 Euros in ten years' time, not to mention inflation. Should I continue? This concept of wasting small amounts of money on a regular basis is also true for people who smoke or have a prestige hobby.

Face your weaknesses and be stronger, than they are. Even if you don't want to give up your daily coffee, beer or cigarette, at least try to reform these habits to fill your piggy bank. If your willpower is strong enough, and you transform this money weekly into your investments, you will see the difference in your account in a few years' time.

If you are young, saving 5 Euros daily means giving your dreams 35 Euros weekly. Within a year you save 1,820 Euros which is 72,800 Euros in forty years. And we are only speaking of 5 Euros a day, imagine if you can save more than that. Of course there are inflation factors, but still, I believe it's better to drink one less coffee than throwing all this money out the window. And you didn't even have to do anything special, besides making a little compromise with yourself.

Remember!

Little changes can make a significant difference in the long run. Rome wasn't built in a day. Building a sustainable lifestyle should be your long-term goal. This is why I am giving you these simple examples to help you understand how small steps and little savings can take you to financial independence. Try to personalize my advice and adopt them into your circumstances. Coffee may be your daily doughnut or the hundredth lipstick. Start controlling your habits and don't be your own enemy. If you stop this little but unnecessary spending, you will gain massive capital.

3. Reduce your shopping for daily items and think in bulk

Buying in bulk doesn't mean that you should run into the shop and randomly buy a bunch of things. Look out for special offers and places where you can shop at wholesale prices, and do not buy the things that you will probably never use just because it's at a good price. Concentrate on items that you use in your household on a daily or weekly basis, like cleaning supplies, bathroom cosmetics and such. Look around at home and make a checklist of what it is that you really need that needs to be replenished constantly, and be very strict with yourself when it comes to shopping.

If you order goods online I highly recommend that you order as many items as possible at once. This way you can save on shipping costs, time, energy, and avoid the stress of running out of things. Of course, you will pay a high amount all at once, but you won't have to go surfing unnecessarily online or do occasional shopping for many weeks, as you will have all you need for months. This way you reduce the number of shipping instances as well, which in turn is also good for the environment.

It might hurt paying 150 Euros all at once, but remember that you would probably end up paying out over 200 Euros if you ordered these items six times instead of once. Also, later on the price of the item might rise. So cherish yourself and buy your favorite fragrance in the big bottle or get 2,000 pieces of bamboo cotton buds at the same time. If you have enough space to store these items you will have more freedom and less stress in your life because you will not run out of them so often, and also you will save money. So make your life easier, my dear, frugal student!

4. Rehome your items

Is there anything at home that you don't need anymore? Please don't throw still usable items in the trash. Go and earn some money. Have a garage sale or sell the items online, or just give it away for free to someone else. Your thrash may be someone else's treasure.

Do you have a friend who just moved into a new empty apartment nearby? If you have two chairs that you don't use anymore, why don't you give it to them? It's a very nice gesture to help someone through bad financial times with this kind of support. Do you have too many books? Sell them!

Buying used things is wallet-friendly, but selling items you no longer use is even better. How many items do you have that you haven't used in years? Shoes, clothes, kitchen gadgets. If you want to find out, put on a note on your things with the date when you last used them. You will slowly realize that the things that you thought were essential are actually not as useful as you previously believed, and they simply collect dust.

There is someone out there with a frugal mindset who wants to get your item at half-price. Deal! Sell it. You will have less to clean and get some money to invest. It's a life changing tip, because when you realize that you don't need so many things in your life to be happy, you will save a ton of money in the long run. Become less impulsive, and slowly you will realize that instead of shopping malls, garage sales offer the possibility of finding what you need at half price. I can't remember the last time I paid full price for clothes, but I have everything that I need, and I am satisfied.

Remember!

Small coins are your friends. Those who don't respect the small coins and simply throw these items out, don't deserve the millions. Be creative and give these items a new life and grab that money.

5. Reuse what you can

This is when the real game starts and things become interesting. I know that as a young woman, I am the target of advertisements that try to influence me to buy anything and everything, but I don't give my money away so easily.

Do you know what I learned from zero wasters? Do you know what they do incredibly well? They reuse everything they can.

I use reusable things wherever it's possible and think in long-term. These are highly affordable opportunities. You can buy washable diapers for your babies, instead of paper towels use microfiber towels in your kitchen for cleaning and also for removing your makeup. You don't have to purchase expensive hairspray. The secret magical serum is nothing else but 200 ml of water with 2 teaspoons of sugar. Buy just one kind of cleaning product or better make it at home on a zero-waste way, cheap and environment-friendly.

Don't be afraid to use your hands!

Before parting ways with old things, first I always consider whether there is a way to up-cycle them. Only a lack of imagination can stop you. Look on Pinterest for ideas. Dear gentlemen, do you really need everything in the garage? Just go out, and find items you could up-cycle.

If you are brave and talented enough then you can cut your own hair at home or dye it or do your nails, learn some new professions and become a jack of all trades. There are brilliant YouTube tutorials if you want to learn something new.

Please only try things that are not dangerous, and you are sure you will be able to handle.

Find recipes with ingredients that you already have at home and make yourself and your family a tasty low budget meal.

6. Repairing and Repurposing your stuff is cool

Tutorials, tutorials and tutorials. Nowadays, there are free tutorials on almost everything online. You don't even need to read instructions because in most cases there are already existing videos on YouTube on ways to repair your items. Surely you need some basic technical understanding, but if you are confident and determined you can do wonders. I have fixed up big wooden chests that were in terrible condition. I repainted them with some old paint and saved around three hundred Euros. Now I have a beautiful planter box for my vegetables. This is what repurposing means. Creativity is essential, and you will see the world through different eyes.

You won't be a millionaire by this method alone, but your creativity will save you a lot of money. Check out some DIY projects on YouTube, you will probably find one to help you repair or repurpose items you already have before rushing to the stores. Check your home for leftovers such as textiles, old curtains, jars or vases, wood or anything usable. You might repurpose these materials and make something beautiful out of them.

However, I want to remind you never to attempt to fix something that requires the knowledge of an expert, such as mending electrical appliances, the heating system, or repairing a gas leak. It's not worth risking your life. There are cases when you have to call a specialist who can manage these issues properly.

Consider Minimalism

Many people choose a minimalist lifestyle nowadays. They want to make space in their lives and more peace in their minds, and also spend their money on fewer things. In my view, minimalism is a way of life where we are aware that our planet is unique, and we need to respect it. Furthermore, we should realize that this planet has finite resources. We should only take the things we really need into our daily lives, and sometimes surrounded by fewer things can make us happier, healthier, calmer, more balanced and less stressed.

Homework

Look at the things around you and consider how much you really need them. Have you ever thought about how much time you spend arranging your stuff? Keeping them organized, washing your clothes or cleaning the dishes or your kitchen. If you add up all the time you spend with these activities, you will see how much time it takes to keep your things organized. The less you have, the less time you spend taking care of them, and the more time you have for yourself. Just think about what else you could actually use that time for.

Many motivational books suggest that everyone should keep their surroundings in order. I suggest that you should have fewer things surrounding you in your house. You will immediately have more time for life. You can enjoy the moment, relax and even use the extra time for learning about financial development, like reading this book. Also, think about all the money you can save. After all, people fill their homes with objects from impulsive shopping, objects that they will literally never use.

Chapter Six

How to turn your pennies into millions

We already talked about what you need to do differently in order to save up some capital, so you can start investing. Now it's time to learn how to create wealth. The first thing you need to do is learn about finance. You should actually start this process while you are saving up your capital.

The internet is full of videos and blogs, where you can educate yourself for free. Learn the meaning of a portfolio, index, Bayesian analysis, history of finance, stock market, gold, silver, platinum, trading, day trading.

Learn what a broker is, which companies are performing well and which are not, what is IFRS, bookkeeping, ETFs, micro and macroeconomics, transnational companies, statistics, real estate investments, cryptocurrencies, flipping goods, or how to start your own business, and how to be well paid in your profession. **In other words, how to be the best financial advisor for yourself.**

When someone handles your money instead of you, like a broker, make sure to have a good wheelbarrow, because you will end up delivering most of your gains to someone else's doorstep.

But you are still asking: *"Ok, even if I learn about finance, how will my few hundred Euros a month in savings turn into millions?"*

The magic of Compounding Interest

Let's say you have a 2,000 Euro monthly salary, you are 20 years old, and for the first time in your life you can manage to save 100 Euros a month, and you want to be a millionaire by the age of 50. The question is, how will you get there? **The answer is, with the magic of compounding interest.**

If you were to hide €100 a month in a box for 30 years, you would have €36,000 saved up, less inflation. It's almost not even worth saving for 30 years, is it?

However, if you deposited €100 a month into an investment account with monthly 6% compound interest earning and compounded monthly, in 30 years you would have €101,000.

And if you managed to deposit a little more, the amount would increase significantly, due to the mathematics of compounding interest.

What is compounding interest, and why is it going to blow your mind?

Interest is the money you earn on your investment. You deposit 100 Euros in the bank. The bank gives you X% on your deposit. The following year again, they give you X% interest on your 100 Euros.

Compound interest is when you earn interest on the money you have invested and then also on the interest you have already earned. In other words, your interest also makes interest.

In time as you earn more money, but live frugally and work hard to earn extra cash, you can gradually increase your monthly deposits up to €1,000 for 30 years, and you will have over a million Euros without doing anything else. But these numbers can change depending on what you invest in. You can find highly over-performing assets, which will earn you higher interests. And yes, some assets will lose you money. The 6% example over time is a safe, expected average.

It will take about ten years to see real results, but everything depends on how principled you can remain. You see, that's when the magic really starts to happen. After about ten years, the interest that you are earning becomes more than the funds you are depositing. Let me say that again in another way, so it sinks in. After about 10 years, your deposit is matched by the interest you are earning. And the interest just keeps growing as time goes on, so eventually it will surpass the amount you are depositing. When you reach the 20-year mark, all the money you have earned in interest will be more than all the money you have deposited over the 20 years. At this point, the effects of the compounding interest will really take off. By around year 30, your earned interest will be twice as much as your total deposits. So, can you guess what happens at year 40? Your earned interest will be three times as much as your total deposits. How about we throw in another decade? Year 50. All the money you have earned in interest is now 5 times as much as all the money you have ever deposited. Imagine teaching your children what to do with all the money they will inherit from you. According to compounding interest, your grandchildren and theirs after that will never have to work a day in their lives. Warren Buffet has once said: *"Someone is sitting in the shade today, because someone had planted a tree a long time ago."* It is time to heed the words of great masters of finance.

How long do you have to keep investing?

Of course, at some point you want to enjoy all that money, and you are going for cashing out on the fruits of your sacrifice after 30 years. Do not worry. If you are disciplined enough to stay on this path, by the time you reach the 30-year mark, hopefully you will have developed such appreciation for value that you'll make the right decisions with your wealth. I doubt if after 30 years if you had that million you would buy a car for 700,000 Euros. Of course not. You'd be sensible. You would likely be able to make many of your dreams come true without spending all of your savings, and you would keep tending to your tree. Now you tell me that it is impossible!

Mastering the right moment

Remaining patient is not always easy, I know. We all want instant gratification, and to live in an instant world that includes love, happiness and money. But how sweet is the feeling if we get our reward after we have waited and worked for it for so long? Mastering the right moment is a significant key figure in being a frugal millionaire. You don't always have to get everything when you want it, because if you do, you will have cash flow issues or debt.

Before I owned my first car, I used to go to work by bus. The company was located 15 minutes away from my home by car, but I took the bus, which took approximately 1 hour and 15 minutes daily. I went to work by bus for about three months. I had to change three buses to get there, and I was always very tired and frustrated. Sometimes I got fed up and was ready to buy a car the very same afternoon. But Gavrilo, who is the ultimate master of patience, taught me a fundamental lesson.

We went car shopping at the weekends, and I tested a lot of them. Since I was very impatient, I was going to buy the first one even though it was in an awful condition and had many kilometers. But Gavrilo helped me overcome my weakness and advised me to wait for the right one.

One weekend at the beginning of July 2017, we saw a car for sale for a price too good to be true. It had been used as *"a weekend car"* by an old man with very few kilometers in it, at an unbeatable price which I could afford without going into debt. As we went for a trial drive, my boyfriend Gavrilo said, it was like a new car and I should buy it. And I did.

I have been driving this car for more than three years, but if I sold it now, I would get back the price I paid for it even though I tripled the driven kilometers. Sometimes I want a better car. I see many people driving bigger, faster and more exclusive cars. But I don't need that unnecessary debt these people take on themselves when you buy a good car at a young age. They often forget it is a liability and not an asset. Personally, I would never buy a new car because as you drive it out of the salon immediately you lose a ton of money. You need to buy the car of your dreams after you worked hard for it, earned it, and you can afford to go with this depreciation. Do not start your life with a giant debt just to impress your environment by driving a beautiful brand new quality car.

"You have to harvest your grapes in October when they are ripe and not in July when they are green and bitter."

This is a philosophy of a frugal person, and always remember that you will get that car eventually, just keep working for it even if you feel that life is short, and you want to enjoy everything instantly. Patience is a key take-away from this chapter. Set new standards for yourself and do it only for yourself and not in an effort to impress others. Financial goals could be influenced a lot by impressing others, so if you feel weak, remind yourself to count to ten, patience will always help you stay determined in your financial goals.

Chapter Seven

Soul before money

Make your health a priority

Your body is your castle, and only you can take care of it. I think the year was 2020, when we learned that our mental health is something that needs special attention. It is not only our physical health that we need to focus on and train in our free time, but we also need to strengthen ourselves mentally and spiritually, so we can perform better. Having enough positive energy is important in achieving our goals and refueling our thoughts and our soul with.

Avoid burnout

Giving energy to negative feelings, worrying, overthinking and stress is never good for you. Financial security is just one part of your life, but not everything. You must be able to concentrate on other parts of your life, too. If you check your account every five minutes, and you are afraid of losing your money too much then it will not only make you frustrated, but you will generate within yourself a source of unhappiness.

I know many people with enormous wealth, but they are constantly running in the rat race. Your mental health and inner peace need to come before money. Running after money senselessly is not healthy or without risks. Burnout, addictions, and depression are serious illnesses among top managers but affect everybody. You should try to avoid them, or they will kill all your motivation and having all the money on earth won't make you happy and satisfied.

Let's talk about burnout. It might be unbelievable, but I had burnout at the age of 24 because I wanted too much at once. Fortunately, with proper therapy, I managed to overcome it within a year. A number of things can cause burnout for me, like self-pressure, being annoyed, stressing and messy colleagues; no perspective of personal development at my workplace and the stress of relocation and becoming an adult.

At that time I was working full time, and doing my Master's studies which meant that I had to give a 110 percent performance seven days a week without taking a break over a one-and-half year period. When I went to work crying every day feeling miserable after being mobbed by two of my colleagues and I finally decided to see my GP to ask for help. I was sent to see a therapist who advised me to change my workplace ASAP.

I was determined to solve the situation in house with my superior, who was shocked by seeing me cry my eyes out and by the disturbing letter my closest colleague had written, which was the cherry on the cake of my burn-out. The HR tried to solve the situation by separating me from one of them, but when I had to replace her for six weeks I was faced again with how unorganized and messy she was, which was exactly the opposite of my organized way of working. I lost all my confidence in her. I could only concentrate on the mistakes she was making and as technically nothing changed I couldn't hold back my frustration anymore, so I left with my last bit of dignity. Although they wanted me to stay and offered me a higher salary, I refused and freed myself from an unpleasant situation. Leaving was the best decision of my life. I wanted to tell this story for all those who can't imagine what a burnout is like. Also, I want to support those who are going through one right now and motivate them to make a change.

Choose wisely

Let's look at an example of a meaningful life-decision, like choosing between two jobs. One of them pays outstandingly well, but there is a second option that would make you feel better in the long run, but pays a few thousand Euros less. You know in advance that you will hate the first job and detest going to work on Mondays, and you'd only choose it for the better salary. Sometimes earning more doesn't mean living better, because your soul should come before money. It's an important key in your work-life balance, which you shouldn't neglect. If you choose a job only for the salary, you have to count on eventually burning out. This condition is way more common than you think, and spending all your saved money on therapy or medical care after working for it so hard is a horrible feeling. Please do not undervalue the risks of this decision. Look for additional possibilities and find something where you can earn well and enjoy the tasks too. With experience, there will come a point when you feel more relaxed and peaceful about your finances if you handle the situation mentally well.

Of course, life is not that black and white. Life offers you many colors of the rainbow and if we interpret it into your finances then, not only advantages and disadvantages exist in one opportunity. It's important for you to learn to handle all the drawbacks, too. Solving issues mostly requires mental toughness, and you can train yourself for it, which will save you a lot of energy.

Staying calm

You might ask yourself right now about what mental toughness exactly means or how you can get it. The first step is to understand that panicking is never helpful, so remain calm at all times even if issues appear out of the blue and all of a sudden. You need to think with a calm mind.

Are you immediately stressed out when your plan doesn't go as you imagined at the beginning? Then the first thing you need to realize is that you might be following a wrong pattern.

Look around your environment and honestly ask yourself: Who in your environment behaves the same way when something negative happens?

Have you ever seen your parents panic when they were in trouble? Or has a friend of yours been extremely stressed before an exam? We learn how to behave from others around us, so please discover this behavioral pattern in your close environment first and try to recognize who influences you the most. Then think about whether this pattern helps you or not to achieve your financial goals. The second step is to find new and better suited patterns and inner peace. You can't start a new habit without stopping the old way of thinking, and you have to constantly keep reminding yourself to adapt to your new lifestyle and not to fall back into the old one. Be calm in your mind and constantly remind yourself. Panic is always bad. With investments, the fear of missing out is always in your shadow, but you have to take your time before an important decision or at least be prepared and invest carefully.

Work when others relax, enjoy your time when they panic

You can learn a lot from school projects, especially when you need to finish those projects on a deadline. Most students want to learn and finish everything within one day, mostly the night before the exam or deadline. It's not only nonsense, but you will not even remember anything the next day, you waste a lot of energy, get no joy of knowledge and stress about failure. Why don't you split your time, learn for an hour every day and repeat it before the exam? Don't be your own enemy.

Memorizing is very important, and you have to sleep to store the information in your brain. It's way easier to recall information from long-term memory than remembering things you learned 15 minutes before the exam. On the other hand, something unexpected might happen and you may have to manage your studies in even less time than you planned. I started to apply a technique in high school. On my way home on the bus, I would study instead of looking out of the window or listening to music.

As an economist I would identify this as a competitive advantage as you are more prepared than your rivals, so you will be way more confident on the exam and less stressed out. You don't necessarily have to be a member of that group of nervous students who endlessly repeat, *"I will fail"*. The same goes for real life and work. If you make a to-do list at work, and you don't leave everything for the last minute, then you will be more organized than 80% of your colleagues. When you are an employee, this tactic will help you overcome difficult and stressful times, just as entrepreneurs also prioritize their tasks.

Life is beautiful

Don't be very hard on yourself and treat yourself by going out and spending some money. Of course, I don't mean all the money you have, but going to a restaurant, a spa or other activities is nice sometimes.

I know you think it might ruin your strict frugal plans, but every frugal millionaire needs some self-time and if you always say no to yourself, you won't be able to enjoy the nice moments of life.

I do believe that you sometimes need to reward yourself, but remember not every weekend should be a big overspending celebration if you want to achieve your goals. Being a frugal millionaire is about balance between spending and saving. Before you treat yourself, remember to do something productive first. It will give you the motivation to keep working and get some rest only once you have achieved your milestones.

Sorry to tell you that if you have friends who like going to the pub every afternoon you might not be able to join them and spend a ton of money every day. You should look for cheaper activities and try to persuade your friends to do so as well.

Chapter Eight

Life Partner And Personal Relationships

Self-development comes before relationships

LOVE is *love*

When I was younger, I spent all the money I got from my parents because I didn't know there were other financial ways to behave. It took a while before I realized I should start saving some money. Learning about savings and how to handle money are not part of the school curriculum, so every young person has to learn them on their own. In long term relationships clear communication is a must and so is setting common financial goals.

Life Partner

When problems occur, do not turn your back on, or be angry with your loved ones, or end a working relationship. Believe me, if you have a loving relationship, achieving financial goals together is way easier. Work on it, try to figure out what works for both of you and create your financial path step by step. Common financial success is hard mental work in relationships. It requires significant cognitive ability from both partners, not to change their personalities and not to become a jerk because of money.

There are a lot of things that can cause difficulties in a relationship when one of the partners tries to build their savings and the other one overspends. If your beloved one is the latter, and you don't like their habit then you have to try to talk with them and explain your feelings and your strategy, and talk to them about your long-term dreams and goals. When the love of your life plans to buy a new car right now, but you know that it will put you in a financial strain then it's time to talk and prioritize.

Communication is always the key to common financial success. Most of us want to belong to someone. If you are thinking frugally, but you are with someone who has no money in their bank account by the middle of the month, you will have issues in the long run. Also remember something important. Never try to buy love for money because it can't be bought. Love is either there or it isn't. Appreciating someone only for their money shows lack of inner value. Your life and relationship shouldn't only be a social medial post with expensive gifts, exclusive holidays, or nice cars to show off. A beautiful picnic with home-made food or going for a lovely evening walk together proves that love is not about money. Nevertheless, having money is a significant part of our lives, and setting and achieving common financial goals such as giving your child the opportunity of an excellent education or buying a vacation home for your old days determines the quality of your relationship.

Financial intelligence is something that everybody can learn, but our paths and expectations are not always the same. Everyone should understand that finding a rich husband or wife is not a realistic life goal. Some people might find richer partners, but most people have to work to fulfill their goals. You may enjoy a relationship with financial benefits, but don't be the person who stays with someone only for a comfortable and easy life, otherwise you will become a miserable millionaire.

Grow up to greater tasks

These three and a half years of my life were like a military training and a mental transformation. There were ups and downs with satisfying and also deeply disappointing moments in it. I had plenty of time to think about what I can adopt from this new lifestyle into my original life. I learned how to handle antique objects of great value and respect things in the long run, to understand how the mind of the rich works and never to put all my cards on the table. I learned patience, thinking with a calm mind and waiting for the right moment, and learned why the masses fear money.

Don't allow anyone to change your personality with money, but be prepared to improve yourself. Learning from somebody who was extremely determined, mind-changing, principled, and organized helped me change my way of thinking. I was criticized a lot at the beginning, but love and understanding from my side helped me through the tough moments.

Learning from someone with great wealth means they will behave in an entirely different way from an average working-class or even middle-class person who never had the opportunity to hold tens of thousands of Dollars or Euros in their hands. Learning from someone, especially from a life partner with a strong personality, is not always the least painful way to learn self-discipline, but it pays off. Compliance and excellence have been a priority for me ever since, and it is also an essential part of the frugal millionaire mindset.

Your financial attitude doesn't only depend on your life partner, but also on other people surrounding you. They influence your thoughts about money, well-paid professions and wealth, and the meaning of being rich. You might feel that you are being pushed into purchasing. But we need to realize that we are the ones responsible for realizing if someone tries to influence our financial behavior unfavorably.

You need to be able to select good advisors from your environment and learn from them. You can recognize them by their entrepreneurial mind even if they are employees. They often have some side business, and they explain their ideas but don't push their thoughts on you. One of my dad's friends is a talented entrepreneur, and he always comes up with brilliant ideas. He instinctually has a frugal millionaire mindset. I showed him an online advertisement for free pickup of hundreds of kilograms of tiny pebbles. Right away he said, *"It would be nice to pick it up, package them in one-kilogram boxes and sell them to aquarium owners."* I was amazed at his frugal millionaire creativity.

If you surround yourself with resourceful people, you will be more receptive to ingenuity and free-minded brainstorming. But be aware not to show your million-dollar ideas to anybody you have just met. Only share your ideas with people you trust, or they might steal your ideas, and it might cost you a lot of unpleasant moments and dollars.

Learn who you can trust

I highly recommend not to explain your financial status to everybody. Money is an everyday topic amongst people, in most cases it's either about a lack of money or boasting about having it. If you want to save yourself uncomfortable moments, talk about your financial status only with people you really trust. There are moments in your life when you have to be quiet. You never know who is a thief or who will try to borrow money from you only never to return it. I heard several stories about nasty businesses within the family and friends in which the trustworthy friend or relative loses their savings. In many cases there isn't any contract between the parties and the debtor never pays back the loan. The biggest loss however is not the money, but the trust in the loved one.

When you have a weekend family gathering years later, the only thing you will think about is why that person has bought an expensive jacket again instead of giving you your money back. But you love this person and would never remind them of their debt, even though you should. Have you ever heard about someone who lent money to their daughter and son-in-law for a business which later went bankrupt? I have a good friend who did so, and she knows she will never see her 10,000 Euro again. If you decide to lend money or talk about your financial plans, then listen to yourself first and stay quiet until you are a hundred percent sure that this person will not abuse your trust. Sometimes people pay what they owe quickly, as I did when I paid my mom back the 2,000 Euros she had lent me within a few months, but this is not always the case.

Friends

The kind of people you surround yourself with matters a lot and highly influences your habits, too. Today, unfortunately, it's more and more common to try to meet the expectations of your environment. You're better off if you surround yourself with energetic people who give you good vibes, think positively and hardly ever complain. Seeing only the negative side of life will significantly deplete your finances. You have to learn that being positive is not about being a superhero and everybody has life issues to deal with.

People often make the mistake of thinking that they have to solve everyone else's problems. There are times in life when you need to focus primarily on yourself. Therefore, you must accept that you will not have a solution to everyone's problems. Not everyone will be pleased to hear your advice, and their explanation and response will not necessarily fit into your life. Be prepared that not everyone will be happy with your new goals and financial success. You are only responsible for yourself and achieving your goals.

Your Environment

You probably live in an environment that expects a lot from you. Most of us are social beings, and we like surrounding ourselves with many people, and we often talk about our goals to them. Remember, we all have different ideas of the world, and we all have different ways of solving problems or hindering tasks. Sometimes people will try to dissuade you from living your dreams. Don't get disappointed if your close environment starts criticizing your plans. Sometimes they can only see the obstacles and the reasons why you can't reach them. Don't be angry with them, and don't get discouraged if you feel that they don't support you straight away. It's not a reason to give up. It could even be your mom who tells you that *"my dear little son, this is surely not going to work"*. But it could also be your beloved aunt, a friend of yours, who you think would support you, but instead they say *"it's a stupid idea and impossible to achieve"*.

You have to keep in mind that these are not your thoughts, so just keep going after your dreams. A positive attitude will drive you further and help you achieve your goals. If you have a goal, then there is a way to get there, you just have to be creative and believe in yourself!

If you have a good idea, then you probably need capital. First, it's your family and friends whom you can ask for financial help. It's possible that they won't understand your idea and refuse to help. Don't get angry with them, it has nothing to do with how they feel about you. A lot of people are afraid to lend money to others, because they might have had a bad experience in the past. So please be creative and find the money you need some other way and stick to your dreams. Of course robbing a bank is not an alternative.

Don't give up your dream just because it takes longer to get there instead of having it instantly. Abandoning your dream is the biggest financial madness you can do against yourself. You shouldn't care about what others say or what is expected of you. There will always be negative comments whenever you step out of the traditional way of thinking. It can lead you to the frugal millionaire mindset.

Homework

Relationships are beautiful, but you have to learn to be whole on your own. You need to work on believing that you are enough and happy by yourself. If you are in a relationship, and you depend too much on somebody else's mood, feelings, decisions, then it will have a negative effect on your self-development. Keep reminding yourself that you are whole, and not half of something.

Chapter Nine

Mistakes to avoid

Learn how to say NO

Now I am going to talk about how not to waste your money, time, and brain cells. I am a caring person and when I was younger I believed I could save the entire world. Nowadays, I know that I have only two hands and, my resources are finite. There are only 24 hours in a day, and you need to make priorities and know what to focus on at any given moment in order to do your best.

You can never change the past, but the future is something you can influence, however, you can only do it in the present. So be present and say no when you feel you can't manage some tasks, otherwise you will make your life extremely stressful. There are moments in life that you can't influence, but there are foreseeable situations that you'd better not be part of. If you go to a meeting and the salesperson wants to sell you some life changing investment, wake up and think a bit before you say yes. You'll be often put under time pressure to make hasty decisions, but you should never fall for it. Remember, they work mostly as entrepreneurs, so they live on commission, so their offer might not necessarily be the best option for you. If you feel that their service or product is not for you, then this should be the moment to say no. Simply said, choose your friends and environment well, learn who you can trust and don't be afraid to say no.

Over the years I have visited several fancy financial events and heard of hundreds of life changing financial opportunities. I am not against young entrepreneurs, companies, and financial advisors. I know many people who trust them, especially those who are not ready to manage their own portfolios. But I believe that there is a cheaper and smarter way to do it. These events are organized to make the sales guys wealthy, not you.

You have to be prepared that at these events they will play with your emotions to seal the deal. The opportunities they offer you always have hidden costs, such as enormous commissions for portfolios or huge entrance fees. You can be sure that the cheapest way is to say no, check all your options first, and try to manage your portfolio on your own.

Once I was invited to a spacious hall where about 50 people listened to a real-estate manager explaining what a great investment it was to buy a 30 square meter apartment at an *"incredibly cheap price"* of €180,000. Besides being extremely overpriced, the project was to be built right by a noisy highway. As it often happens at such events, it was presented as a life-changing opportunity to become part of their team as a financial advisor or as an entrepreneur in the MLM system. Of course, having had previous experiences, I knew there would be a catch. So I stayed until the first break, had a lovely dinner and went home with a full stomach and pocket. The others stayed and listened with glistening eyes, not realizing that their money would soon disappear from their wallets.

You've probably heard stories about lottery winners who have lost all their fortune in the blink of an eye because they didn't know how to handle situations just like this, and how to manage all the money.

Don't put all your eggs in one basket

The key figure in investments is very simple: Learn to diversify your portfolio. What does it mean? It simply means that you are able to divide your wealth. So you don't risk all your money in the hope of gaining on some risky financial assets.

Building a portfolio is not only helpful but a must-do if you want to retire rich. Even if you own a small amount of money at the beginning of your journey, you need to know how you will organize your finances when you start your savings. Do not put all your saved money in one thing, because you always must have your plan B, C, D, E, F, G, and so on.

If you put all your money on your plan A and the market becomes unfavorable for your investment, then you have become your own enemy. At this point, I must mention that there are some businesses where you see a massive opportunity, and you might become greedy, but this behavior often leads to failure. I heard several stories about people spending all their savings and buying one stock or putting all their money into building a new business which ended up going broke. Many self-employed people go through tough times because they don't realize what their limits are. This is one of the reasons why so many people don't dare to enter the self-employed playground, because they are afraid to have these harrowing experiences.

Getting through hard times

There are unwritten rules and occasions in everyone's life when your ability to adapt yourself becomes a significant factor. Going through hard times might not only cause financial issues, but could be mentally stressful as well. In these kinds of situations, choosing the right path might not be easy. Making hasty decisions under stress is never a good idea, so I highly recommend that you figure out some alternative plans. In finance there are dangers and if you put all your eggs in one basket, you are taking on an extraordinary risk.

Before making a decision ask yourself whether this kind of risk is really necessary in your life, or is it reckless, and if you are willing to get into the new situation without the security that had surrounded you so far in your life.

I am not encouraging you to fear life but to live it with sense. A single misstep can destroy your invested energy and money, which can be heart-breaking.

Surely there are some good ways and opportunities to invest your money, but do not risk your entire wealth. Sometimes you have to be brave, but always set aside some money. The amount you need to put aside depends on your lifestyle. If you own your home, then you don't have to create reserves for rent expenditures. However, you have to account for emergencies, like replacing a washing machine or a boiler that might break down in the middle of winter.

It is also important to take your debt into consideration if you have any. If so, you have to calculate it in, to be able to pay your debt for a few more months. There are other expenditures as well such as food, insurances, services, medical care and so on. Please remember that your own emergency package is never part of your investments, it serves you to overcome situations like losing your income for a few months.

Homework

Now is the time to calculate how much money you'd need to upkeep your current lifestyle for another six months.

Know your boundaries

Not every investor is the same, and we think differently. Even if you are not familiar with investments, you should learn about them for long-term success. There are key books and authors on this topic, but if it's your first time typing *"investment"* into the Google search engine, then you might get shocked at the tremendous amount of possibilities you'll be faced with. Don't rush if you are not sure, and don't put your money into the hands of any broker before you are entirely sure that this is the best solution for you.

Are you a risk averse, risk neutral or risk loving individual? This is an important factor of your frugality. The more risk averse you are, the more you are afraid of losing your money. But if you love risks and don't get sleepless nights if something goes crazy on the market, then maybe crypto is the best space for you. How we take risks is personal, and you can't compare yourself to anyone. There is a well-known example among economists about two brothers. Peter has 1,000 dollars and Paul has 100,000 dollars. For Peter one extra dollar has a higher value than for Paul, therefore one additional dollar is of higher utility for Peter.

I can't tell you what you should do with your own life or which kinds of businesses and exact portfolios or numbers you should achieve. As I have already mentioned before, we all have different ideas about what wealth and being rich means. It depends on several factors like your location, your expectations or your opportunities.

The above explained risks and tactics are significant factors to remember. Understanding yourself is a learning process, just like your priorities and how much risk you are willing to take for them. Learn to avoid the risks you are not ready for and take care of your portfolio just as birds protect their eggs.

To achieve your goals it is important to remember to be able to say no, not to put all your money on one card, stay strong through hard times and be doubtful if you hear about an investment that sounds too good to be true, because not every investment will produce a thousand percent returns like Bitcoin did.

Envy and Long-term habits

I love to talk about how we should handle money in general, but in this chapter I need to mention one more important topic related to money and long-term habits. The first time you'll earn large amounts, you will get some questions from your family and relatives.

Money is often something that people connect with negative energy, and you might not want to explain your success to them. You will usually get criticized if you talk about your goals, mostly from your close environment. You need to understand that we have different stories and life situations, and not everybody will support your goals and congratulate you on your success.

Please remember this effect will be more substantial if you are surrounded by people with scarce resources. If you explain your goals, and you behave too enthusiastically or show your success, you might be on the receiving end of negativity or closed ears.

Trying to impress others might kill your plans

The next mistake is that you want to impress others with your money. One of the biggest enemies of a frugal millionaire is trying to impress your family or meet their expectations once you've collected some capital.

Buying a bigger house, a bigger car, going on expensive vacations and giving expensive gifts is now your possible playground.

This will hinder your further financial development, and you might want to wait for a couple of more years. Sure, you can do what you feel is the best for you, but remaining a few more years in a low-budget lifestyle might help you achieve much bigger financial success.

Even though you gain capital, you need to keep your old frugal habits if you want to remain a millionaire. Remember that 90 % of lottery winners lose their entire wealth this way. You shouldn't feel like you had won a lottery, because you worked hard for it, and keeping and growing it is a long-term job.

Gavrilo told me many stories about Ms. Annie. There was one which inspired me a lot: One day she asked him to buy some frankfurters from the local market for 0.99 cents, just like she had been doing every week for years. When he brought it to her, she smelled it, and it was awful. She told him to go back to the shop and to ask for a refund. He was embarrassed to take the meat back, so he threw it away and bought a new one for her. When he got back, Ms. Annie said, *"You didn't return it, did you? You just bought a new one, didn't you?"* He said, *"Yes, I was ashamed to return a 99 cent item in a Mercedes."* She got angry, that he was willing to lose money in order to maintain his image. He finally, for the first time, understood the principle of the frugal millionaire mindset. Never try to impress anyone with your money, it is the worst thing you can do. You will see that people will disappear from your life because they are only part of your life to fulfill their interests.

Chapter Ten

Szakonyi's Frugal Millionaire Cake

What does a portfolio mean from the frugal millionaire mindset perspective?

The normal financial explanation of a portfolio is a cake that is divided into slices, each representing a different financial instrument. I approach the cake a little differently, so we can call this the Szakonyi's Frugal Millionaire Cake. Let's assume you are a hungry kid, and you've just got a cake. Your cake is divided into 5 equal slices, and these slices will make your stomach full and turn you into a financially responsible adult. You are a child who wants to become a millionaire within 20-30 years, and you already know that success is not born overnight.

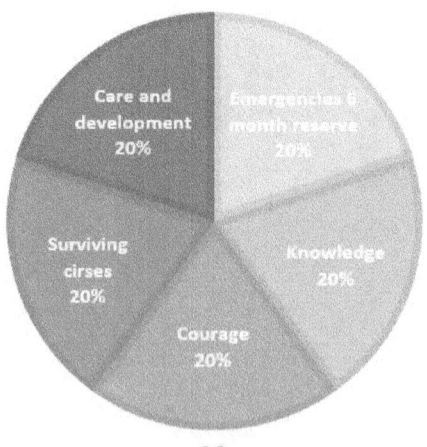

1. Emergencies: 6 Month Reserve

The first slice. Cash that is not tied up in your portfolio, in case of emergencies. You need to have enough so that if you lost your job, you'd be able to pay your bills and have food to eat for 6 months. Very few people have a 6-month reserve, but this is the first step to financial independence and to becoming a frugal millionaire.

The lower your monthly costs are the less this 6-month reserve has to be. And you can reach this amount sooner if you keep your expenses low. This is where you can use the lessons about zero waste. This is the most important slice to survive, because if you do not have this emergency fund, then you won't have the peace of mind to invest.

90% of people will never finish the first slice, therefore they never get to the second one, and they remain on the hard way of learning finance. You need to define your necessary reserves and create them. I know it sometimes takes a long time, but you need to start step by step. A little success is still success, and do not fret, it won't take forever. You need to take an honest look at your expenses and see what you can cut from your monthly list.

2. Knowledge

The second slice is knowledge because without knowledge you can't invest with confidence. This is the time to practice the easy way of learning. Yes, you could invest by giving your money to other people to manage, but do you remember the wheelbarrow example?

You have to develop yourself and learn about finance because if you don't, you will have no idea what is going on in your portfolio, and you will be overcome by fear. This is the slice that you should never finish, because you must be willing to learn for a lifetime. New opportunities will emerge, and you must stay alert and open to take advantage of them. If you have updated knowledge, you will be able to view new options that appear on the market with a critical eye.

3. Courage

The third slice is for being brave. Conscious planning is the active investment of money and the definition of a portfolio. Step into the field of action by setting up a plan, and stop waiting for a miracle to happen. This means that from now on we invest a certain amount in a certain form every month without finding any more excuses and fears. Fear is weakness and weakness is over with this slice, and you need to bravely take responsibility for your own life and be proud of yourself.

4. Surviving Crises

The fourth slice - Surviving Crises - This slice of the cake is not as delicious as the first 3 slices, but you can only reach your path to financial freedom and the frugal millionaire mindset if you eat this slice too. This is the most significant slice.

Again, you can only do this by pinching from slice 2 and knowing what the risk is that you can bear and what your risk taking attitude is. You can eat the 4th slice much easier if you eat the first one carefully, and you have your emergency funds behind you.

People who do not eat the fourth slice- meaning, training themselves not to give up when crisis hits, often sell out of panic.

This usually happens when they have invested too much, and they imagined that everything would go up forever. In most cases after a market crash everything recovers, it's just that these people sold at a very bad moment because of their fear of losing everything, and not being able to hold on and be patient during a crisis. You must think in long term and need to ignore the momentary hysterical market behavior and the fear of the masses.

5. Care and development

Care and development - Becoming a millionaire by portfolio. It's not just about money, because money doesn't make you happy in itself. It includes personal development, the realization of goals, your family, life partner, joy, and real desires, which is why you chose this cake in the first place. The cake of the frugal millionaire mindset is not always tasty, but these simple ways will give you long-term confidence.

I know many of you expect immediate results, and I'm sorry to disappoint you, but financial success comes at a price, which is staying on the path that is paved with time, with your perseverance as your fuel.

Chapter Eleven

Prioritize and focus

Write down your ideas

Many of us make a very simple, but significant mistake which seriously hinders our financial development. You can easily manage this issue in a simple way. You need to start writing down your own ideas before you forget them. The making of a to-do list in order to see your ideas on paper is necessary to record your brilliant ideas, and also you can check them a few years later, too. You have to write down your best ideas, because these are your assets. Have you ever been in a situation where you had a good idea and five minutes later you had already completely forgotten what it was? Your notes can help you a lot to increase your creativity and this could be a useful tool to earn more capital on the long-term.

How to prioritize

Do you start things that you never finish? You have a thousand ideas, but you never put them into practice, or you take on 15 projects at the same time? These extremes are the reasons why we do not achieve our goals. Many talented and creative people fall into the mistake of bringing up new ideas constantly and working on several projects at the same time. They start a process with extreme enthusiasm, but as the next idea comes into their minds, they lose focus of the old project. In this chaos they often lose motivation and when the next good idea pops up they don't start it because they already know in advance they will be unable to achieve them in real life.

What can be done?

How can you focus your energy on one project and take financial advantage of it? It is not always easy to make the right choice. If you have several potential business ideas in mind, then you might lose control and switch between ideas.

Eisenhower Matrix

I think one of the best tools to make you successful in decision-making is the Eisenhower Matrix; Make Urgent vs. Important Decisions with 4 Quadrants.

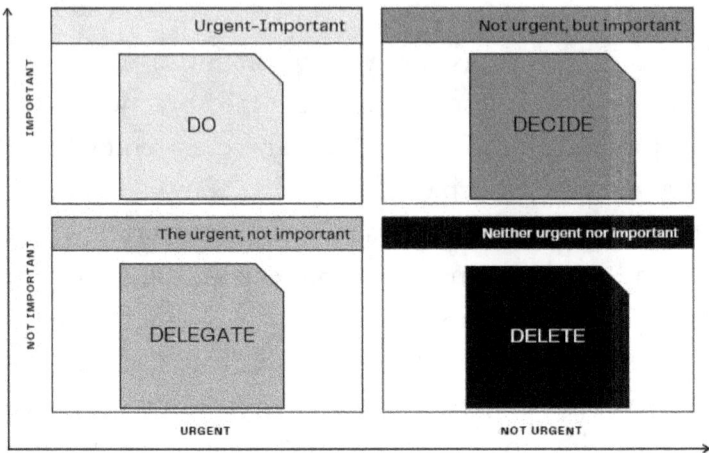

First, you have to come to terms with your own priorities. This matrix is often used by top-managers in decision-making, and you can easily adopt it into your life.

Homework

Take your notebook or an Excel file and create your very own Eisenhower Matrix. Below, you will find the instructions and some help on how to do it. If you truly believe in your personal and financial development, I would recommend you to make a list on a monthly basis, a yearly basis, a three yearly basis and on a five yearly basis, too. So you need to create four different matrices. This way you can get a clear overview of your plans and ideas, and you will make your development much easier. Please include all of your personal and financial visions, ideas, hopes and definite plans for the future, and don't be afraid to dream and think big and step out of your boundaries.

This matrix has four parts, and now I will explain how to work with the sections separately.

1. Section number one is the Urgent-Important box.

In this box you write down the urgent things which are also important in everyday life, work, finance, personal development etc. What is really urgent and important to you in these fields? You need to decide what you personally find urgent and important. Think for a moment and answer yourself. Technically this is your basic project, your main financial goal you work for and things you literally must do and can't avoid.

Make it your priority to work on these urgent-important tasks every day. Remember, goals and issues are at the top of your priority list.

Here is an example. You hate your job and it pays badly. So, it is urgent and important to do something about it. It is not enough to write down that you hate your job, but also that you want to change within one month to improve your situation. Stay calm and don't be hasty. Quitting without a plan and waiting for miracles to happen is not the solution. You can write down in box number one that you hate your job and what you need to do to solve this issue. For example, write an updated CV and apply for multiple jobs to change your situation faster. You also need to define your steps, because without a manual you can't follow through your plan.

2. Section number two is the not urgent, but important box.

Here you start the real planning, because you have already defined your highest priorities in the first box. Ask yourself, which things are really important to you, but can be postponed. To achieve your most desired dreams they have to be moved from box two to box one and give them deadlines.

We have thousands of dreams, and we hope we can achieve them in the future, but these dreams never come true if we don't move some of them into the urgent-important box. We tell everybody about these dreams, but we never fulfill them, we think we have enough time, and we hesitate to start. But if you really want them to be realized you need to come up with a definite plan and a deadline.

Let's say that you want to improve your financial knowledge, but you don't do anything to achieve this goal. Come up with a personal plan and be strict with yourself to keep to it.

For example, watch thirty minutes of videos about bookkeeping or read thirty pages on this topic every day for a year. Don't miss any days, don't complain, and do it even if you are exhausted, bored or have had enough. This principled behavior will help you become someone with the frugal millionaire mindset. You won't be able to realize all your dreams because we all have too many of them. Pick your most important dreams and start to do something about them.

Never put them off until tomorrow, otherwise you will never feel successful. If you never fulfill any of your dreams, and you already missed all the possibilities life had given

you, at the end of your life you will stand there with bitterness. I know these are painful words, but they are true.

3. Section number three is the urgent, not important box.

Here you need to start delegating tasks and becoming a strategist. Decision-making is a key to organizing your tasks, finances and goals. If you have the possibility to give some of your tasks to people who can help you out, you can concentrate on your first box.

Think of a boss who doesn't do all the jobs necessarily single-handed. He has employees do them, while he concentrates on the strategies and primary goals.

Let's look at a simple everyday example. There are so many time-consuming tasks that take your attention away from your real goals. You should take a serious look at your life to see where time flows out of your hand. Does your shopping take hours? Are you on social media all day long? How many favors do you do a day? You are a boss who simply doesn't manage tasks optimally. You think that having food at home, checking what happened on social media or doing favors are urgent. But at the end of the day, it was you who couldn't achieve the goals from box one.

Most people don't define this box correctly. You need to do these things in your personal life, but improve your skills. Why don't you shop online once a month to save time? Why don't you check social media less often? Don't be afraid to sometimes say no to favors when you really need your time for yourself. You need to be able to concentrate your energy on the really important things and on yourself. It's part of your self-management strategy. It doesn't mean you are selfish, it means you are principled.

4. Section four is the neither urgent-nor important box.

It's time for spring-cleaning. You should decide what is not part of your financial and self-development plan. Take a minute to see which things, people, habits, everyday tasks annoy you, rob you of your time and energy or simply linger around you, unnoticed. Yes, you heard well. You should put some people here as well, people who you wouldn't like to meet anymore or listen to them telling you about their miserable life for the hundredth time. Don't let them suck the life out of you and make you dead tired after a half an hour conversation. It's time to be harsh, even if this person is one of your family members.

I know it is extremely hard and painful to let go of things, people, habits that once made us very happy. Nevertheless, you need to make room for better things, positive people who motivate you. Don't forget with old, out of date patterns, mindset and habits it's impossible to achieve the frugal millionaire mindset. As you already know, this book is not only for financial but also for self-development.

Unfortunately, without making the necessary changes there is no personal development either, so do it for your own sake. I know it is very hard. Once you have finished the spring-cleaning, you will realize that you actually have a lot more time for urgent and important things than at the beginning.

Chapter Twelve

You have earned your money, what's next?

If you have been diligently investing for a decade or a few, depending on how much you have invested and how well you have managed yourself, you may feel that you have arrived at your destination. But then again, you might not. You might want more. If you want to continue earning with your investments, it is very important to continuously summarize your financial goals. Are you moving towards your goals, do you have new ones? Is the road you are on actually good for you? Are you just a small fish in your market, or are there bigger things you can accomplish occasionally? Are you just treading in stagnant water, perhaps? Find out what the reality is. These are tough questions, but they need to be examined to have a clear view.

I know many people who reached the peak and became financially independent, and they are still unhappy because they never understood a very important lesson.

Money is an efficient tool, a part of life, but it can never be the goal of life.

There are some people in their 40's who have built their careers and have reached financial success, but they have spent their entire lives chasing money, and they have failed to find themselves real goals in life that brings true happiness, and even though they are wealthy they are still unhappy.

In most of these cases, these people try to improve and increase their levels of happiness by looking for physical pleasure. We often hear about sex scandals of successful business people, or if they are elderly and their sexual activity has decreased, then we hear about ways they exercise their power over others and being tyrants. Of course, this pattern is not only true of recognized successful business people, but we have all heard about their examples. This behavior has a lot to do with their inner being, because they have been only running after money for so many years.

So how can you eliminate these bad patterns and become a happy millionaire?

1. Find real values in your life. It could be your partner, children, family, hobby, a pet, an organization or anything else you can live for.

2. Personal development, but mostly develop your spirit and soul.

3. Respect other humans.

4. Find yourself a noble goal. There is nothing to live for if there is nothing that motivates you to fight for something again and again with renewed strength every day.

5. Never stop using your frugal habits, stay proud of them.

6. Don't let your environment change your habits.

7. Remain your own best friend.

8. Live for your passion.

Non-material elements

Financial success also has non-material elements. As a social being, you can help your own mental health and that of other people if you are in a better financial position.

Be there for other people and embrace people in a challenging life situations or give them financial help, or maybe work for an organization. Most successful and financially over-performing people stand up for a greater good. You can be one of the people who practices the habit of generosity. If at this time you do not have the opportunity to financially support an organization, it is not a problem, but go and do some volunteer work.

Help distribute food to those in need, help out at an event for free, do some shopping for an elderly person, or do something that will drive you in that direction. The more you give, the more will flow back into your life, both spiritually and financially. You will also establish valuable relationships in your life. Also, you will find a lot of joy in activities that help people who have half as much confidence as you do.

Chapter Thirteen

Lessons Summary

We have arrived at the end of this book, but before you close it, let's take a look at what you have learned. Please take these last pages with you as key takeaways. In the future if you only have a little time you can read this summary to refresh your knowledge about the frugal millionaires' mindset. As I have mentioned several times in this book your time is your most valuable asset, so this short summary is created for you to use later.

Whenever you feel stuck, this chapter might help you overcome your frustration and help you remember what it means to have a frugal millionaire mindset. Enjoy it!

Let's see the key points from each chapter.

The Hard Way of Learning Finance

You must eliminate all bad patterns from your life, if you want to be successful in finance. Bad spending habits, negative outlook on life, wasting time on unproductive things, failing to learn from the mistakes of others are all things that will hinder you from staying on your path.

Easy way of Learning Finance

You must find your passion, and have a crystal clear idea about what you want to achieve. Write down your ideas and always keep a positive attitude, especially about your goals and dreams. Learn from the mistakes of others, save yourself a lot of grief and time. Always stay calm when making decisions and build your reputation by being reliable.

Take control of your spending

Live below you means by saying no to frivolous spending. Lots of tiny amounts flow out of your wallet daily, if you don't pay attention to your everyday lifestyle habits. The money you think you don't have to invest is right there in your pocket, you are just spending it in the wrong direction.

6Rs

Rethink / Respect everything around you.
Refuse to spend on all that is unnecessary.
Reduce your shopping for daily items and think in bulk.
Rehome - give items a new purpose/use.
Reuse - eliminate single use items that add up to a lot in the long run.
Repurpose -create new useful items from things you already have.

How to turn your pennies into millions

First you need to gain basic knowledge of finance and investments in order to be able to invest on your own. Remember, you want to skip the agent, so you can keep all the profits! When you have a clear plan on what you want to invest in, you need to commit to your decision long-term. With continuous deposits into your investment account, over the years the compounded interest you earn will inflate your earnings significantly.

Soul before money

A lot of ambitious people fall into traps like working too much and burning out, or choosing something you don't enjoy, just for the money. Take care of yourself, and realize that money isn't worth anything if in the end you are a stressed out mess.

Life partner and personal relationships

The people you surround yourself with deeply influence your life, sometimes even without you realizing it. Sometimes the friends we already have may not understand your new mentality and plans. Avoid discussing your plans with people with negative mentalities, and find the people that understand you and will move ahead with you.

Mistakes to avoid

There is a lot of opportunity for sale out there. And whenever you come across them, you can be fairly sure that they are traps. Do not hand over your cash to be a part of anyone's system. Do your own system and remember if it sounds too good to be true, it probably is. When you invest, don't panic, and don't share your successes with the wrong people.

Szakonyi's Frugal Millionaire Cake

This cake consists of all the elements you need in order to invest with confidence and live a fulfilled life.

Prioritize and focus

Take control of your dreams by making a financial plan for yourself. Write down everything you need to do, and prioritize your tasks using the Eisenhower Matrix.

You have earned your money, now what?

Your journey never ends. By now, you know what time can do to investments, so it is smart to keep investing. Enjoy your money but stay humble and live for a noble goal that will truly make you fulfilled.

Closing thoughts

Time passes so quickly. A few decades may seem like a very long time, but as many older people will tell you, it passes in a blink of an eye. The financial mentality you live your life with will determine whether you'll thank yourself later, or live in bitter regret. Start using the Frugal Millionaire Mindset today and be on your path to success. Now is the time to become the best friend of your older self, to offer comfort, security, and peace of mind. It will be the most rewarding friendship of your life.

www.ingramcontent.com/pod-product-compliance
Lightning Source LLC
Chambersburg PA
CBHW070657220526
45466CB00001B/482